Becoming #heavenlyMindedMomma

FINDING THE GOLD IN HEARTSMASH

ALANNA KING

TWO REALMS PRESS

This book is a memoir. It reflects the author's present recollections of experiences over time. Some names and characteristics have been changed, some events have been compressed, and some dialogue has been recreated.

Cover design by © Victoria Heath Silk

Cover photo by © Sean Lavalsit

Cover textures: © Unsplash.com

Author photo by © Photos by Kayleigh King of Wild Kind Photography:

www.wildkindphotography.com

Interior Formatting: Shari McGriff

Ornamental image: Flatiron.com. This image was designed by Adam Kelly.

Printed in the United States of America

ISBN Print: 978-1-7335358-4-7

ISBN Ebook: 978-1-7335358-5-4

While some publishers and Bible translations use lowercase for the name of God and His pronouns, the author has chosen to capitalize God in all sentences and quoted scriptures, regardless of scripture translation. This capitalization aligns with the author's style and is applied consistently throughout the book, which also includes the word Glory, as It is God's presence. Take note that the name of the enemy of our souls and related names are not capitalized. We choose not to acknowledge them to the point of violating grammatical rules.

Becoming #heavenlyMindedMomma

This book is dedicated to my children, Gian, Belle, and Zosia, and to their children and their children's children. May the words I've chosen to share on these pages further convince you of my fierce love and dedication to each of you, forever. May you be drawn to the Source.

Contents

Foreword xi
Jack Little & Katherine Walden

Introduction xiii

1. November 6, 2015 1
What to Do When Crushed by a Wave
"Wallflower Hero" 10

2. Hope, Kindness, & Grace 19
A Note on Regret
"Choose Light" 27

3. Anne's Prayer 35
We Belong to Each Other

4. Posture Of Forgiveness 43
Releasing to Justice & to the Love of God

5. That Moment In My Unzipped Heart 61
He is Giving Me Beauty for My Ashes

6. Transformative Love 73
Intentionally Living Toward Legacy

7. So Much Joy! 87
My Laughter Had Been Changed by the One Who Sits in the Heavens and Laughs.

8. Addressing The Court 101
Ignorance Doesn't Protect; Nor Does Fear.
"A Return to Civility" 111

9. Second Chances Or Mercy Versus Nineth Chance 117
Unsanctified Mercy and Life as Free Will Agents

10. Victim Panel Statement 125
"I Have Three Children."

11. Finally, A Dream! 141
"I've cashed in My investment." Father God

12. Making Every Moment Matter 149
Just Love the One in Front of You

13. Surviving To Thriving 157
Clarifications on Grief, Loss, and Trauma

14. If Jesus Were Sipping Coffee At My Sink 173
Would Jesus Say That To Me?

15. "It's All Gonna Be Okay." 181
...Like Honey to My Dry Toast...

16. Notes From Year 8 195
...Is it ALL OK?

Afterword 211

Resources of Companionship & Joy 213

Endnotes 219

Acknowledgments 225

About the Author 227

Foreword

JACK LITTLE & KATHERINE WALDEN

As a pastor and church planter, I believe there are lessons to be drawn here for all of us who need to face life's hard blows due to unexpected loss and heartbreak, as we try to make sense of it all. Our hearts are set on making sense of the beauty that arises from the ashes, as Alanna King has experienced. Alanna brings a unique hope to those who need understanding, and she offers us a path. This book ***is*** a healing place.

~Jack Little

Church planter and founding pastor, along with his wife Kathy, of *Kingdom Culture Prescott,* and eight other churches. Jack has trained and sent out over 30 pastors and teams to plant churches in the United States and Canada. He also served as National Regional Coordinator for the Association of Vineyard Churches for over 15 years.

Alanna and her family's life came to a screeching halt the day that their beloved Gian was taken from them. I understand the jolt of impact all too well, having lost a beloved brother just as suddenly. In this book, you will find some hard truths, laughter, joy, and frank anger. You will also find an unshakable faith in God and the God who held Alanna's family in the midst of devastating gut-wrenching, heart-stopping pain.

This ***is*** a book that offers hope and encouragement, sympathy, and empathy. It's not one that hides behind platitudes or wraps up grief with a nice little bow. However, if you are going through grief, you will find comfort in knowing that somebody else is having the same thoughts you have and is fighting the same battles you face. If you are walking alongside someone on a grieving journey, much like what Alanna's family, this book will give you insight and tools so you can be of true help. You'll be invited to set aside unbiblical presumptions on forgiveness, grief, loss, and letting go.

I admire Alanna's unflinching honesty, vulnerability, and courage as she tells her family's story. This book contains wisdom and carries a light that will help you navigate through those really hard seasons of life. May the Father of all Comfort guide you through the dark nights. He promises you that joy will come in the morning, and I can reassure you, deep abiding joy will come!

~Katherine Walden,
Author of *Not Always All Together, Dare to Call Him Friend,* and *Seasons: Reflections on Changes Throughout Life.*

Introduction

PLEASE COME SIT WITH ME...

Influence is when you are not the one talking, and yet your words fill the room; when you are absent, and yet your presence is felt everywhere.
~ TemitOpe Ibrahim

When our eighteen-year-old son, Gian, left for Heaven, much of me left with him. I didn't just lose my son; I lost promises, at least earth side anyway. All of my hopes, dreams, anticipations, and expectations of our shared future, every personal and professional relationship of mine, every perceived ability or skill set, and each step of my daily routine, right down to breathing, have been completely turned inside out (by inside out I mean at one point early on after coming home from the hospital without Gian, I could not remember how to spit, so I swallowed my toothpaste). Along with everything I've believed about my God, our legal system, what freedom really means, the power of our choices, and what an accident is and what an accident is not, while I am technically still me, I now stand one foot on the planet and one foot in Heaven, the pre-crash me has been radically reconstructed and has the capacity to hold the tension between Heaven and earth. I would never have imagined.

Some things we endure alter our perceived trajectory at a cellular level, and trying to share my version of life before and since November 6, 2015, feels like a huge responsibility. I desperately want to honor Gian, our family, our friends, our community, and our very good God (Who's graciously taken insults and accusations without retaliation), who is not to blame. I want to make Gian proud of his momma. I will always fight for him and for my girls. Our girls, G's younger sisters, have been there experiencing it all. They've watched all the details unfold before their young eyes. Gian belongs to them. Our beautiful girls...lost their innocence and youth. Initially, I thought coming home that Sunday without Gian was the hardest thing we would EVER do. Not true. The very hardest thing we would ever do is continue. Every morning, we awake again to the realization that Gian doesn't live on the planet anymore, make the decision to get out of bed to endure the demands of life in America by the grace of God (and much like a marathon runner), only to return to bed at night with the realization that we'll have to traverse another day of life apart from our G again.

Having expressed that, believe me when I say I am NOT a theologian or a scholar. I am, however, a daughter, a sister, a wife, a mother, a friend, a coworker...I will not wave my bible at you; I do not believe I can speak for anyone other than myself. I will only put to words what I feel complete permission to share. I will love you, though. I will do my best to not hurt you in my own hurting.

My hope is to stir deep, deep moves of goodness through my invitations to lean into my "what happened" for the sake of experiencing the greatest personal good possible through one mother's love for her son and daughters, through a healthy interpretation and journey of grace in the midst of the most painfully powerful life I've been thrust into.

Goodness, defined by Merriam-Webster, is "the quality or state of being good." Good is defined as "something conforming to the moral order of the universe. Advancement of prosperity or well-being." And well-being is "the state of being happy, healthy, or prosperous." [i]

We know that for those who love God all things work together for good, for those who are called according to His purpose.

—Romans 8:28 *ESV*

MAKE NO MISTAKE; THE GOOD I REFER TO HAS TO BE **MASSIVE**. The kind of massive that comes to mind, which could only be satisfying to my heart or might have the possibility of answering my devastation, would HAVE TO ripple out way beyond my comprehension and tangible appreciation. This kind of goodness will have to go far beyond the limits of my sight and impact so many hearts that my own heart would become so full, to the point of overflowing and be so heavy with goodness, that it'd have no other option than to respond by rolling over in its weightiness and do something like a tap-out, "OK. OK. That's too much goodness, I can't take it anymore." So, the goodness that I am demanding because the bible says I can, does include you. It has to.

The goodness coming to me will look like you feel as if you are seen, loved, deeply cared for, prayed for, encouraged to keep breathing...and hopefully experience some ease in your breaths. It's OK if you don't believe that my kind of goodness can overtake your life; I will believe it for you if you need it. Rest in my hope for you.

I get to keep loving Gian, regardless of where he lives. It feels very true to direct some of that love and encouragement to those of us who find themselves living without someone they never intended to be apart from.

God knows other Moms, Mommas, Mamas, Mommies, and Mothers who have helped to love me to life over and over again. This book is written with them in mind. Your wholeness will also ripple back to them because we are far more connected than we understand.

Most of my life I've struggled to find and then finally use my voice. Curiously, it is in sharing my loss, grief, goodness, and the gold that allows me to hold space for others' shared experiences. Years ago, I attended a Saturday workshop at our local community college. Seventy-five or so of us gathered to earn an additional two credits and learn a few more things under the *Organizational Leadership Resource Management* umbrella. At some point during the day, the professor instructed us to get up from our chairs and choose a place to stand along the walls of the room. Facing the center, we were to turn our attention to a chair. The professor then instructed us to take in each detail and study every aspect of the chair's curves, colors, and textures to recognize any interesting features. We stood with our backs against the walls in silence for more than a few minutes, just soaking in all we could.

From our unique places along the wall, we were asked one by one to share as precisely as possible, as descriptively as we could, what we were seeing.

This exercise changed my life in immeasurable ways as I listened to the individuals around the room sharing what they saw and experienced. Some of us determined that the paint on the chair was green until the people standing with their backs to a window saw it as blue. Incidentally, these same classmates started to sweat and fan themselves as the sun beat on them through the window while I shivered with the air conditioning vent directly above my head, just across the room from them. One guy read aloud a statement scratched into the backrest of the chair that the classmate on the opposite side of the room had no idea existed until they listened to someone else's observations. Of course, there was gum stuck to the chair, but I could not see it myself from my place on the wall; someone else had to tell me about the size, color, and imagined consistency of the blob. We all agreed we were looking at the same chair, yet every single one of us had our very own experience of it. Some of us were overheating. Some of us were freezing. One of us chose to do a wall sit instead of standing to give their back a break. My back was fine.

Our professor interjected again with questions like:

- Is it wrong for the chair to be blue?...
- Is it right for the chair to appear green from another side of the room?...
- Can both observations be accurate,
- or can both observations be factual?
- Which color is right?...
- Is there a wrong way to see the chair?...
- Why are you standing where you are?...
- Is it possible for someone else to precisely share what you are witnessing of the chair if you choose to not speak?...
- Is it a kindness to invite the cold folks to stand in the sunny window, and if so, will you invite them?...
- How does the lighting where you are standing affect the way you see?
- Do you wish you were standing somewhere else?...
- Do you want to escape what you are experiencing and deny it altogether?...
- Is discomfort distracting you from focusing?...
- Does anger or frustration prevent you from seeing at all?

Some of these questions could have been in response to the body language of a few of the students. Not all of us were participating. Not all of us valued the exercise. What began as declarations of descriptive statements developed into a conversation as we discovered how unique our experiences of this one chair in the same room truly were. Many of us became eager to know what we weren't seeing instead of being determined to define and defend our views. We grew curious about what the others were seeing and feeling. Within just a few minutes, respect and freedom to rest in my own spot on the wall unfolded in an unanticipated way as my classmates shared, contributing to a fuller understanding of the chair. Each of us had something to add. I realized that if I wanted more information about the gum, I only needed to ask the person who could see it!

I felt validated and peaceful as clarity washed over me. I finally got it! I felt permission to tell my story while providing a welcoming heart and space for others to share theirs with me. Every one of us has a vantage point from which we can provide a piece of the fullness of the shared experience of life. My place on the wall is just that. Just my place to give voice to, to be descriptive, and to offer support should someone else find themselves suddenly experiencing life like I am. A dear lady, Gian's elementary teacher, said the other day, "None of us make it." At some point, all of us breathe our last breath. Let's talk about it now. Let's dig up fear and throw it out with the weeds. Let's please set our differences and assumptions about loss/people/Heaven/God aside and choose to focus on all that is lovely, pure, honest, and true. The reality is we belong to each other, and we are all going Home.

In this book, **I will do my very best** to be who I am and give voice to what it has meant for me to begin to thrive. I wasn't sure I would survive at all, much less thrive. What a lofty, depending on the moment, offensive insinuation that thriving is even remotely possible following the traumatic loss of our son.

Yet, here we are, thriving out of wreckage is something I will, no doubt, be leaning into for as long as I am on the planet. Thriving will look different for all of us. For me, thriving includes honest tears, acknowledging my heart, being patient with myself, and choosing kindness while celebrating that not all losses are equivalent. While I have experienced great loss, balancing the scales of loss or trauma is not up to me. What is up to me is deciding to be a conduit of Love. Maybe that's your goal, too. Sharing our story is only part of loving well. While I love the idea of the whole world knowing Gian's name, I absolutely crave the earth-side version of wholeness, thriving, and well-being for everyone, especially the mommas of the world who have endured the unimaginable.

I have become determined to make death regret ever messing with my family by allowing hope and joy to rise again. Fear has lost its grip on me.

Until I am all wrapped up in Gian's arms again, I will live out my minutes determined to thrive organically, to watch Heavenward, to stir hope, allowing my own hope to be stirred, to anticipate Love getting His full reward in me, through my loss, through the strikingly beautiful life of our son Gian. I'm fully anticipating striking beauty in exchange for my ashes. Telling my story is part of all of that.

Come sit with me. As I share my story, my prayer is that you will find comfort, companionship, hope, some healing, some wholeness, and more peace. It could be that gratitude, joy, glimpses of gold, and glimmers of Heaven will increasingly catch your attention if they aren't already. If you have an ash heap like I do, may the audacious transparency of our evolving beauty encourage your own evolving and increasing beauty, too.

If things have gone horribly wrong for you, please know you're my kind of person, and I'd love to hear about your scars, how you're caring for them and your heart, and the people you love too, wherever they are.

All Love,

Alanna

P.S. I love the idea of learning about ourselves as we learn about those around us. While I've attempted to paint a vivid, honest picture with all the words I've chosen through this book, the picture is incomplete. It's impossible to tell the whole story in one fell swoop, or at least within roughly 50,000 words. Yet it's important to begin the conversation. As the conversation unfolds, even if the communication is simply happening between me and my pen and paper, the truth is clarified for me, most importantly.

At the end of each section, you'll find a prompt for personal application and conversation. In my opinion, the best conversations are simple, easy, and honest. Just bring you.

You are the best gift there is.

Finding the Gold

Heartsmash is the term I created in an attempt to form words describing the condition of my heart and soul following the death of our son. If I had the honor of joining you at your kitchen sink to share our lives and learn about you, I'd first ask about the Green Chair in your own life.

What is the central, big thing you are focusing on right now? Who are you celebrating? Are you grieving? What are you learning about life, yourself, or as you walk this journey?

How is your place on The Wall impacting your perspective on the Green Chair? How have your loved ones' perspectives impacted you? Do you recognize aspiration as part of your Green Chair experience along the wall? Is there room for goodness to be drawn into and through any brokenness, disappointment, or heartsmash?

ONE

November 6, 2015

WHAT TO DO WHEN CRUSHED BY A WAVE

To my family and friends,
you make life worth living.
~ Gian

(penned the fall of G's Senior year of High School. It has since been tattooed on his youngest sister's forearm.)

Years ago, when our family was whole, a friend shared a podcast with me. Something encouraging. I don't remember who the speaker was or much of the message, but when he (I do remember that much) talked about being desperate for advice during a challenging time in his life, he went to Google for help. When asked, "What do you do when crushed by a wave?" Google answered, "Have peace and float to the top."

When I heard that phrase, I immediately knew I had to *have* it, and I quickly jotted the words onto a scratch piece of paper, shoved it deep into my purse, and promptly forgot about it until that weekend. This kiss from Heaven would work its way to the top of my purse to reintroduce itself as it became clear that we needed a miracle, and as it became clear, there was nothing for us to do, nothing we COULD do but to have peace and float.

It doesn't take much for my heart and mind to be right back to the moments of our last Friday with Gian. I wonder if he knew. I wonder if getting out of bed that morning felt different to him and a bit more precious? Easier? Did he linger in his sheets? Was he eager to live out his last Friday on Earth?

I distinctly remember a trip to Costco after my workday. The normal items were on my grocery list, and among the usual items were lunchmeat and granny smith apples for Gian. I alternated between smoked turkey, peppered turkey, smoked ham, and roast beef. Only this time, as I stood in the deli section, like I had probably a hundred times before, specifically for lunch meat, I could not physically bring myself to take any of the perfectly great sliced meat options off the shelf to put it in the cart. It was the strangest thing. As hard as I tried, I couldn't do it. Same with the apples. I stared hard at the apple display, only to walk past them.

When I arrived home without the lunchmeat and apples for Gian, he was standing in the driveway happily talking with two young men that I hadn't met yet. They were busy loading Gian's motorcycle into their truck for a test ride over the weekend...yet the air around Gian was golden as he engaged his friends with his incredible and vibrant full-faced smile and laughter. GOLDEN. The air around him glowed with glimmery, even sparkly warmth. The hue was one I hadn't seen before and could only be described as golden. And I recognized it!

He communicated with the young men with such peace, ease, and joy. He had zero concerns about leaving the bike with them, and it was clear he wanted them to have fun with it. I later learned that the young men were his coworkers.

Once inside the house, he flopped down on the couch to watch TV or play video games. He had been working full-time as a pipefitter since August of 2015 at Puget Sound Naval Shipyard for the Department of Navy, and after a full and labor-intensive work-week, he was ready for some downtime...Gian was between vehicles as he had just sold his truck so that meant he didn't have his own transportation, but his dad and I encouraged him to work out the details so that he could attend the 4H end-of-season award celebration with his buddy Maric like he had a handful of years prior. We just wanted him to spend time with some of his favorite people. The added incentive was that Gian's girlfriend was also going to receive some awards, and with a little finagling, she was able to shift her own plans and pick Gian up on her way to the event. Time was pinched, but everyone was happy to shift a little so that Gian could attend. He quickly got ready, his girlfriend arrived, and as Gian turned to run out the front door, his Dadio yelled, "Kiss your mother before I kick your teeth in!" This quote was from *So, I Married an Ax Murderer*, which Dadio often said. At his Dad's orders, Gian back-stepped and planted a huge and powerful kiss on my right cheek and said, "I love you, Momma!" And out he went. No hesitation.

Through the lens of "I should have," regret is right here when I interpret my own curious moments on this last Friday with Gian. I should have paid more attention to what was happening in my gut, Holy Spirit, or mother's intuition. I should have let him stay flopped out on the couch. A friend once suggested that the Holy Spirit had protected us from watching Gian's lunch meat and apples rot in the fridge. That it was actually a kindness, not a warning or a hint that I had missed. I wonder if the golden hew around Gian had something to do with Heaven being so close and ready to receive him.

We only have a few pictures from our weekend together at Harborview Medical Center. Admittedly, I had gotten lax in my photo-taking as our children grew. Not because I stopped believing every blink, move, and smile was amazing, but because I still want to catch it all especially those big life moments. I have been trying not to miss the moments by letting go of capturing them, and in the course of being "with" them, I've captured less. I treasure every rare moment we get to be together. My heart is to be with the people I love in the precious moments that become our memories.

Part of me understood that taking pictures that weekend meant something big was happening. Something maybe life-changing was happening. Something really important was happening. I was afraid to give a photo my acknowledgment that today might be all we have left and that we needed to "capture" these final hours just as we had memorialized Gian's first hours on Earth. I regret that now. Even though I don't have an image to hang on the wall of my lips on Gian's left temple, my lips remember the feel of his precious skin. That'll have to be enough.

While many moments have stayed fresh in my mind's eye and feel just as vivid when I allow myself to revisit those sacred hours, I do wish we had captured more of them. Friends, our local family, and family from out of state and even out of the country, as well as teachers, classmates, and coworkers, came to be with Gian. Some of them entered our small circle for the first time that weekend and remain in our lives to this day. Heart connections were forged that have sustained us much like chest compressions sustain a stopped heart until it can hopefully beat on its own.

This would also be the beginning of the great good that would flood our lives.

I write these words recognizing that Gian's dad, his sisters, each grandparent, uncle, aunt, cousin, and his friends have had unique experiences with him and because of his life. I don't want to overstep and assume great good met any of them when Gian left for Heaven or since. Nevertheless, this is an absolute reality for me. Painful as the physical separation is, goodness entered my life in massive ways the day Gian was born, increased during his 18 years here, and seemed to multiply the day he left for Home. His life has had a vacuum effect, and his exit from Earth began to draw to us what had been held by his physical presence on the planet. I began to actively look for the gold coming from our son's life. Gian's gold has been easy to find!

On Friday, November 6th, 2015, Gian was life-flighted from Harrison Hospital in Bremerton to Harborview Medical Center in Seattle, following a "collision," and our lives changed while we weren't looking.

From the *Kitsap Daily News*:

SERIOUS FIVE-VEHICLE CRASH AT KITSAP AND NATIONAL IN BREMERTON

> BREMERTON – Three people were injured, one seriously, during a high-speed nighttime five-vehicle crash at the intersection of Kitsap Way and National Avenue at 9:06 p.m. Nov. 6.[i]
>
> — CHRIS TUCKER, NOVEMBER 7, 2015, 2:11 A.M.

I found out later that we were gifted the opportunity to have this additional time with Gian because one of his best friend's grandfather was at the crash site working and chose to order a life flight rather than declare him dead at the scene. We didn't know about this gift until several days later.

Truly, Gian was never more beautiful than when he was wheeled out from the ER in the Bremerton hospital. This was the first time I saw him following the crash. Aside from being unconscious, the tubes filling his mouth, the wires attaching his body to the machines, and the staff surrounding him, there was nothing obviously wrong with Gian besides the medical equipment and the clear sadness all over the medical staff. OK, so there was a lot wrong, but I was really only focusing on Gian and in the fact that he had such joy ***in*** his face! That's the only way I can describe what I was seeing. **Joy was IN him** and shining out of him. Gian was literally glowing with such joy and peace...Now I understand that he was already in the presence of his Savior. I didn't understand what I was seeing at this time. I simply marveled at his radiating beauty. He looked to be in complete bliss. I've not seen anything like it before or since.

We had just a minute with him there outside the ER before he left on his one and only helicopter flight. I nuzzled and kissed his face, rubbed his forehead, and reminded him of my love. I asked him to please try, and no matter what, I was (still am) so proud of him.

Jeff and I drove to Seattle to be with our boy, numb to what all of this could mean for our son and for us. Our minds and bodies could not even begin to comprehend what had happened, what was happening. I remember recognizing that my body had gone completely numb. Although I sat in the passenger seat of our Toyota, I seemed to be floating. I couldn't feel a thing. This sensation was only somewhat alarming as my mind could not wrap itself around any concrete thought aside from the understanding that he needed a miracle. Somehow, I just knew Gian needed a miracle. I began to text prayer requests for just that. No other words were available as I had no understanding of the extent of his injuries, how humanly impossible recovery was, what had really happened, or having any clue what our future held.

...Just hours before, we watched him leave our home, with his girlfriend, so vibrant and ALIVE. Surreal.

We arrived at nearly midnight and were met by my brother and sister-in-love, a niece and her sweetheart, and my parents shortly after. Just minutes later, the medical staff informed us that there was nothing they could do for Gian...he had sustained catastrophic damage to his brain. They were "so sorry." The hemispheres of his brain had been separated, his C1 and C2 dislocated, his ocular nerves severed, he had at least 3 massive brain bleeds in the initial scans, and sustained damage to his liver. His injuries were unrecoverable, and the Brain Death Protocol had begun.

This meant we had just 48 precious hours left with our son. These 2 days were full of tests to confirm what the brain scans and initial tests indicated. The swelling of his brain due to the impact had caused irreparable damage. I remember the sorrow in the doctors' eyes and my intense need to be with my kid. I still have that need. To me, the words the doctors were saying only confirmed that Gian needed a miracle. We had become (still are) bright, flashing targets for God to do what only God can do. I only wanted to make room for that. Having seen miracles before, I was and still am confident in God's love and ability to heal, restore, recreate, and pour Heaven's resources out on the impossibilities we faced that weekend and that we continue to experience each day.

I wanted to be as close to his ear as possible, so I pulled a chair next to his hospital bed, sat on my knees, and leaned in as close as I could to express my deep love, sharing all the ways he had made me proud. I did my best to share my excitement for his future, whatever his future held. I reminded him that his sisters needed his presence. He had been such a good big brother. I told him that we needed his presence. My lips stayed long on his left temple that weekend. I soaked him in my love, kisses, prayers, hope, and tears. What an honor to watch as many, many beautiful people came to do the same.

One of our nieces had been traveling the globe and happened to be home with her sweetheart, visiting her parents. She was able to spend long minutes with Gian in these final days. This gift of time together felt like a kiss from Heaven. Her brother was able to fly in from Oregon. Another cousin came from Australia to be close, to believe with us for the miracle we needed. My sister came from California. Another Sister-in-love, who normally doesn't bring her phone to bed, happened to have her phone with her to answer Jeff's call for help. She and her hubby left their beds and came to be with our girls in the middle of the night, caring for them the rest of the weekend and getting them to the hospital on Saturday and Sunday. Dozens of friends and their families came and stayed from sun up to late in the evening to feed, hug, and support each other and us. I've never seen anything like it and will always remember the generosity of their presence.

The world stopped for me that weekend. My focus sharpened in a way I hadn't known before, where minutes expanded and felt long, where Gian's heartbeat and breaths were all that held my attention...and our girls. Up until that point, none of us had experienced anything so devastating, destructive, confusing, horrifying, unifying, beautiful, honoring, or humbling, and I was desperate to keep my eyes on their brother, just as much for them as for him. He belongs to them. He always has, and he always will. It was as if the dial on my heart was turned way up to be present in every second. I wanted to be with him in all of it.

Initially, we were allowed two people at a time to be with Gian. Within just a few hours, that restriction was lifted, and as many of us that could fit around Gian's bed were allowed in the room. His visitors overflowed the room and filled the enormous waiting room down the hall, as well as the couches and nooks through the connecting hallways. In fact, some of the loved ones present at Gian's birth joined us that weekend to love on him as we waited. I've been so honored in motherhood and had no idea that our sweet boy touched so many hearts. Gian's friends, so many of our daughters' friends, our friends, and family came to just be with us. To just be present. The kindness of presence will stay with me forever. Presence is such a selfless, powerful gift.

The RNs were incredibly kind and EXTREMELY patient with us.

. . .

GIAN RECEIVED CONSTANT ONE-ON-ONE MEDICAL CARE. I can only imagine how difficult it was for his doctors and RNs to answer our incessant questions and to be watched so closely. Every time they performed a brain death protocol procedure, we leaned in closer, probably uncomfortably close for the medical staff, and would cheer Gian on out loud! When they tested his pupils, I would talk to Gian about how beautiful his eyes are, that he has such good pupils, and that we wanted his pupils to react to the stimulus. I remember saying, "It's OK, son. There's another test in a few hours. I believe in you, I believe in your pupils, I believe you can get your healing from Jesus and show us!" So many tests—tests hoping to detect signs of life, probing nerves, reflexes, watching for any response. So many scans, x-rays, blood draws, and infusions. He was only apart from us for about an hour while the last brain scans were performed. I wasn't permitted to accompany him this time. As persistent as I was, the medical staff wouldn't allow it, although I had never missed an x-ray before in his life. The results of his final scan were not shared with me.

At one point, his RN paused, looked me in the eyes, and said through her tears, "I have never seen such love."

In response to witnessing the tender care provided by Gian's RNs, the following poem, "Wallflower Hero," was written by G's sister, Belle. Her words provide incredible insight into our girl's heart. G, as we call him, was her first companion, playmate, confidante, defender, and partner in crime, and he could do no wrong in her eyes—except maybe for the time he hid in the bushes by our front door dressed in camouflage and armed with an airsoft rifle to scare her first boyfriend. Said boyfriend was only trying to say goodbye. Still makes me laugh! (No shots were fired, in case you are concerned about that.)

The following poem is for all the RNs who've taken care of our loved ones.

"Wallflower Hero"

BELLE

We all knew you were there.
It wasn't a party; you shouldn't want to join
You were there the whole time
But I would never be able to point you out in
a crowd
Yet we wouldn't have gotten far without you;
The Wallflower Hero
Thank you for all you have done
Even though for you, it was just another day
Those three nights I will always remember
You, too, the faceless woman
The Wallflower Hero.
It's all over now
At least for me
Because even with your help,
He still had to leave.
And you are still there, helping someone new
With another's eyes passing over you
Stuck in the daze like I was,
And forgetting to thank you;
The Wallflower Hero.

THE MEDICAL STAFF WALKED THROUGH THIS EXPERIENCE WITH us. They endured it with us, and I pray the love that RN witnessed has stayed with her, ultimately drawing her to the source.

Like many times in life with my son, I made space in my heart for his miracle. Allowing that space was the simplest, truly the easiest, most natural response to the impossibility we were facing. Without a miracle, Gian wouldn't be coming home with us, and I wanted my son to come home with us.

Several doctors and specialists came to see him. Most of them were kind, letting us know that they were aware that the patient they were discussing was loved and that we were listening. Yet, a young female doctor sat down by his bed and seemed annoyed with my hope. She sneered at me as she repeated Gian's injuries and the outcome the tests anticipated. I remember looking her in the eyes and saying, "Sometimes it's good to be wrong." Miracles happen when they're needed. I only wanted to keep the flashing "Miracle Wanted" sign plugged in with my hope. I was hoping against hope.

She didn't appreciate my response, and I told her that if she was going to keep talking about my son that way, she didn't need to come back. I didn't see her again, but I've wondered about the condition of her heart.

She spoke as though she'd been talked out of or maybe even relinquished her hope...maybe hope is too risky for her. Sometimes, science doesn't support our hope.

- Hope doesn't and wasn't denying current reality.
- Hope is not ignorant or blind.
- Hope extends the possibilities beyond what is naturally possible.
- Hope is the expectation of good.

God knew we needed something that went way beyond what was humanly and medically possible. Not unlike the time Gian's smashed foot was suddenly restored and pain-free, with only a bruise remaining. Or when Dadio's shoulder was miraculously healed following a simple prayer of faith, and Belle's perfectly healthy lungs despite the damage they sustained as a newborn from severe RSV, and how Zosia survived my complicated pregnancy and an emergency c-section despite my doctor's expectations.

I remember clearly how divine intervention also showed up as protection for Gian in response to death threats he was receiving from a few schoolmates. He had witnessed a drug deal during an assembly in school, and after a lot of thought, he decided to report what he saw.

Although the Police Officer who handled the incident promised to keep Gian's name out of the reporting documents, it was fully disclosed in the court proceedings. The boys were furious when they were finally released from Juvenile Detention and allowed to return to school. They repeatedly threatened to kill Gian over the course of several days. In my opinion, the school wasn't responsive enough, and yet Gian insisted that he wasn't afraid, although the threats continued.

While praying about what was happening with the threats, I suddenly *saw* Gian's back as he stood on a small hill, the sun shining in front of him, completely engulfing him. As he stood unmoving, with his back to me, people walked past him in all directions. Suddenly, huge white wings appeared and wrapped all around him, hiding him. And just like that, the threats stopped as the boys began to fight each other. It was as if Gian was suddenly invisible to them.

I am just a regular, actually very average person with average-person-faith who loves a very good God. Jesus paid for our healing, protection, and real-time help long before we were born.

That's when miracles happen.

At one point during that November weekend in the hospital, I asked Gian if he would go get his miracle and come back to finish his life here. He was living a really beautiful life.

Despite being completely unable, medically speaking, to answer questions, move his head, or respond to any stimulus at all, Gian shook his head as if to reply "No."

I froze.

Two years earlier, we prayed similar prayers for my friend Shiela's daughter, Ally, and I remember Ally kicking my praying hands off her motionless feet. She had gone Home in her sleep the night before. I imagine Ally welcomed Gian home, too.

A couple hours later, on that Saturday, brave friends (Ally's momma, aunt, and uncle) came specifically to pray for Gian's miracle. Ally's uncle was at Gian's right side while her aunt and I stood at the door and began to pray. Again, he shook his head "no." With wide eyes, they turned to me and asked if I saw it. I saw it, too.

My sense was that Gian needed to decide for himself: to step over to the other side or stay with us. The choice was his to make. I only use the word choice because it's the closest to what I am able to comprehend on this side of eternity. We have raised our children to think for themselves, to "make happy choices," as we used to say. Gian was facing into Heaven, and I KNEW this was what I had birthed him for. My heart ached recognizing his natural life; his future was not for me to decide, but for me to watch and see what he would do, just like we had done for the last eighteen years of his life. Not all of us are long on the Earth. (Please see "Anne's Prayer" in Chapter Three.)

Sometime on Saturday, I learned that the woman responsible for the crash (Ms. M.) and her infant son were released from Harrison Hospital in Bremerton. They were fine. I remember how relief washed over me as I received that update. Such good news. It is a curious thing to hold the tension between what is and what will be with grace and gratitude. There was no effort involved in my feeling grateful that she and her son left the hospital fine. That part was easy. In the weeks to come, we would be thrust into a steep learning curve as we were introduced to the concept of calculated risk and collision versus accident.

Late Saturday, one of Gian's medical team instructed me to lie down. While it was excruciating to peel myself away from him, one of his favorite cousins and my sister settled in at his sides, each taking a hand. They assured me they would stay with him through the night.

I hadn't slept since the Thursday before and imagined a nap could be helpful. I worked hard to be still on the little couch in the waiting room, and as I began to drift off to sleep, bagpipe music seemed to blast in my ears! Of course, there wasn't anyone actually playing bagpipes in the hospital that night, but the sensation was jarring and SO real nonetheless!

Incredibly loud and shocking! With that, I returned to my perch at Gian's side.

As the sun came up Sunday morning, I asked to assist the nurse with Gian's bath. She seemed surprised by my request. I don't remember what she and I talked about, only that we did share a few words. I can tell you that extreme sweetness filled these moments as we washed his beautiful body. The same boy I grew in my own body and birthed, nurtured, cherished. It was such an honor to help care for him this way. It's really something to have been part of his first and final bath. I simply could not have imagined anything like it. Incredibly precious.

As our hours grew short on Sunday, organ donation was offered as an opportunity for Gian to live on through the lives of others. A few very courageous family members joined me in exploring that opportunity for him, and I imagine Gian is disappointed with my decision. He and I will hash that out someday. Truly, I simply could not allow it. Undoubtedly, some of our loved ones would have preferred otherwise. I can certainly understand that, as I have family members and friends who have benefitted from organ donation personally. It is an immeasurable gift that saves and improves the lives of people who are hopeless, aside from receiving a miracle of their own. Receiving an organ from a donor is a miracle in itself. However, Gian needed the opportunity to come off of the machines first, to be given every opportunity to surprise us all. Had it been an option for his heart to stop completely on its own before harvesting his organs and tissues, I may have been able to agree to it. My boy lived a generous life, and he wasn't done (in my opinion) living, not done giving, AND he was never mine to give away.

Having declined organ donation, just one thing remained—to be with Gian, to soak in his last minutes, his final heartbeats and breaths, earth-side, to watch as the machines were first silenced then turned off and the tubes removed from his body. We invited family in the room to witness his freedom from the machines and share the hope that he would then take a big breath on his own again. My hope was that Jesus would send Gian back to us whole. My hope was that Gian would be completely healed of every one of the injuries he sustained. My hope was that he would open his eyes, maybe even yawn, and stretch his muscular arms out like he would when waking from a nap.

And Gian is whole. More whole than he had ever been in this life and in such freedom now. Though not in the way I hoped.

Though only blurry, I remember leaving Gian's body as his nose began to turn blue. I have no idea how I was able to let go of him, to walk out of the room and leave him there. Years later, our youngest daughter told me that she had stayed there with him after everyone else had left. She didn't want to just leave him alone and didn't understand what was happening. Eventually, his nurse explained that it was time for her to go, too, and that they were going to keep him there.

I wish I had climbed into bed with him then. I wasn't done loving him, caring for him, or being with him. The floating sensation continued as I hugged and thanked the medical staff for their kind, beautiful care. On our way out, another nurse stopped me, taking my hands in hers. She made me promise that I would say "yes" to the help that was coming. She didn't let me go until I promised I would. I am grateful for her wisdom and her heart for us in her firm instruction. Saying yes would prove to be one of the hardest, most humbling exercises of my life. And I believe saying yes provided pathways for kindness, goodness, and compassion to flow through some of the most unanticipated avenues. God knew we would need some massively good GOOD to flood us if we were going to survive the loss of our son. The good has been massive, and we aren't satisfied yet.

From Liza P. November 9, 2015:

There are no words that can express the emotions properly, but I will write a few that are on my mind.

Yesterday is forever imprinted on my heart. Observing the most beautiful, amazing group of family and friends love on their boy, hoping and praying for God to give him a miracle. I was praying so hard and believing in the miracle. I begged God not to take another beautiful, young soul from this Earth. People we didn't even know, who didn't know the King family, came up to us in the hallways and asked to pray. There was so much love and hope. If love could have saved Gian, he would have been healed.

The loss of a child can never, ever be understood. There are no words to describe the pain. I will never understand why Gian was taken from his family.

I feel cheated not having the chance to know Gian. I only knew him in passing, through many good stories and through the love of so many people that I love, including Jackson. I feel blessed to be by my sister's side yesterday and to be given a moment to touch Gian's hand and thank him for the beauty he gave this world. I was surrounded by a portion of his beauty, his family and friends, at that very moment.

My heart is with the King Family, Stevens Family, my sister, and so many of you that I love, who love Gian forever.

Please know how loved you all are. Gian will never, ever be forgotten and will remain in our hearts and memories forever.

Blessed are those that mourn, for they shall be comforted.

—Matthew 5:4

Jesus said that.

Bless you, those of you who have walked a loved one Home and those of you who have suffered other kinds of heavy loss. May moments of kindness and beauty be highlighted to you as evidence of Heaven's investment and involvement in your life and in the lives of your loved ones.

Finding the Gold

Have you suffered a heavy loss or walked a loved one Home?
Tell me about them. Tell me what happened.
I'd love to hear about the people you love.

TWO

Hope, Kindness, & Grace

A NOTE ON REGRET

Regret is an enemy of our souls and
wants to get us to blame ourselves
for what the enemy did ***to*** *us.*
~ Alanna

I'm not going to lie; **I still have that hope**. I still want Gian to return to his life here with me, with us. Although so much has changed, I want him to walk through our front door and head straight for the fridge. I want him to hug me a little too tight and kiss me hard on the cheek. I want him to drop down on the couch and tell me what he's been up to all this time. I'm eager to hear his excited and rambling stories—his laughter and his joy, and although I miss him—terribly—I choose to live in hope and not regret.

I still have hope.

Regret is designed to eat us from the inside out, and it is eager to eat us.

Regret wants to immobilize and disempower us. Don't let it.

Regret wants to talk us out of believing that God is good.

He is actually LOVE.

Don't believe the lies...

Regret is an enemy of our souls and wants to get us to blame ourselves for what the enemy did to us. Anytime we see killing, stealing, and destroying,[i] we can be assured that it's the devil. Don't let him trick you into blaming yourself or God for his work.

Not one of us can go back in time, undo what's been done, or control the future. There are no magic prayers. We can be sure of one thing; we are born for eternity, and thankfully, life on Earth is not the sum of it. And here's *THE thing*; God never promised us a pain-free or lavish life. He only promises to be with us, and He has a way of turning our ashes into beauty.[ii]

MASSIVE GOOD BEGAN TO SHOW UP IN UNANTICIPATED and overwhelmingly beautiful ways.

Here enters Great Kindness:

It saved our lives. I highly recommend receiving kindness and then pouring it out liberally on those around you. Just as the nurse made me promise to say "yes" to offers of help in whatever form, kindness began to show up before we could say yes. We arrived home that Sunday evening, to find all the fallen leaves from our massive Magnolia had been removed and the whole front had been swept, the fridge was full of ready-to-eat food, and our home was cleaned. The whole house.

Once inside the door, the first place we went was to Gian's bedroom, where I dove face-first into his dirty laundry basket. The four of us found such treasure in his unwashed clothes. Finding fingerprints on his t-shirts was enough to make me praise God that he chose not to use a napkin after so many years of pleading with him to please stop wiping his hands on his shirts! And other treasures like holey socks, or signs of life, as I called them—caught our attention. A week or so later, a heart-shaped dirt clod showed up near the front door. Because we thought it might have come out of

Gian's work boots, we left it there for a long time. Heart shapes began to show up in grease smudges in the garage, coffee splashes, and crumbs on the counters, rocks, clouds, leaves, and in bird poop on the beach! Incidentally, our cat Schmoo also had a *yes*. Upon our return from Harbor View Medical Center, our once very reclusive and bristly-haired boy (kitty) emerged from under a piece of furniture, suddenly affectionate and incredibly soft! His fur literally changed texture. He remains changed today!

The yeses manifested as meals that were faithfully provided for roughly a month by both friends and people that we didn't know yet. Often, the meals were silently dropped off at our front door. There was always more than enough...plenty for Jeff and me, the girls, AND any friends and family members who were present at the time of delivery. Some meal deliveries evolved into rich conversations and long, warm hugs that centered so perfectly on our beautiful son, our daughters, and our hearts. We felt incredibly cared for and were deeply humbled by the generosity, thoughtfulness, and effort so many lavished upon us.

Bouquets of incredible flowers—so many flowers that lasted supernaturally for weeks and weeks covering every table top of our home. Incredibly kind cards, gifts of all kinds, handmade blankets, and items with Gian's name etched, sown, or painted on them began to arrive in hopes of providing comfort while speaking to Gian's impact on the giver. We have it all.

While we aren't *stuff* people, these tangible gifts of love and care arrived at just the right moment. Just when we were sinking hard, feeling breathless and stunned. We felt that way for a very long time. We still do some days.

One evening Gian's supervisors from Shop 56 came to gift us the items in his locker on the base, which included a green apple sucker, his issued hardhat, and his handwritten notes. The shop also presented us with a beautifully framed shop logo that had been signed by many of his coworkers. While these gentlemen conveyed their shock and clear sadness, they also shared how much they liked Gian and appreciated his work ethic and desire to work hard. I especially love that Gian was liked and respected.

I didn't know that we *needed* any help or that we would be comforted by anything, and I am still so grateful other people did know! I can share with you in complete certainty that we would not have eaten if the food hadn't arrived warm, and our attention desperately needed to be drawn to the love our community was pouring on us. Their love and kindness sustained us. TRULY.

At one point, someone looking for a meal prep idea asked me what the girls might enjoy...actually the question was, are the girls eating? The answer was not really. So this Dearheart made homemade cookies, which ended up being the perfect meal for our heartbroken princesses. (It's OK to just get the calories in every now and then.) G's sisters had been so crushed and in utter shock that even eating was physically challenging. For me, getting to the next minute felt like an overwhelming undertaking and a commitment that I didn't know if I could keep, but a homemade cookie was enough to keep us engaged! As it turns out, homemade cookies are powerful.

And money came.

Personally, I really enjoy giving. Receiving hasn't always felt comfortable or easy. Money really did answer many things as we managed Gian's end-of-life expenses and as I ran out of leave at work. I was initially granted 1 week for bereavement, but as you might imagine, there were many more days when I couldn't hold myself together for more than just a few hours at a time. Our income went down as our expenses changed dramatically for a time. As the four of us began to experience the effects of *complicated grief* and *trauma*, the need for our own support became super obvious, and our medical insurance did not cover all that was necessary. As an example, we discovered through blood work that one of the girl's mineral levels had extremely and alarmingly tanked. The doctor said he didn't understand how she was able to function, much less walk, at that time. As we acclimated to regular physical pain, sleeplessness, GI issues, and inability to focus, read, or comprehend while missing Gian, we needed a lot of extra support, and the financial blessing made caring for each other possible.

Just six months later, friends, community members, and a local church joined forces to help us get our home ready to sell because living with empty spaces and routinely driving through the same intersection of Gian's collision became unbearable. So many generous hearts gave of their time, ability, friendship, creative ideas, sweat, heavy equipment operating skills, and hugs to make that relocation possible. It took a village for us to make that change, and we could not have done any of it without them.

The transformation of the home our family of five shared was completed on Gian's 19th birthday. We chose to celebrate him by being surrounded by some of his favorite people. Celebrating him has always been easy, and we recognized how he brought all of us together. We barbequed, shared Gian's favorite dishes, and told stories of him. Just before sunset, our friends and family joined us on the lawn, under the open blue sky, to sing *Happy Birthday*. Each of us with a balloon in hand containing handwritten messages to Gian, sang our wishes to Heaven. As our song was completed, we released and watched as the dozens of eco-friendly balloons quickly caught the breeze and were whisked away high into the sky and out of our sight, except for my Dad's balloon. It seemed to refuse to leave him. He and the balloon just stayed on the grass as if struggling to let go of the moment. Finally, after what felt like several minutes, the balloon began to lift slowly and wag back and forth before finally lifting into the sky to join its friends. (I do have a picture of that.)

And we gave, too. The blessings, kindnesses, gifts, supplies, and support we received have further spurred our own giving. We gave Gian's belongings to his favorite people, to our favorite people. Things like memories, messages, photos, sweatshirts, stained t-shirts, a bow with arrows, a heavy bag or two, his workout equipment, furniture, and used deodorant sticks had become highly prized items. We wanted to share these treasures with G's loved ones, and it felt very right to gift these personal items to the people in the photos who created memories with him, were present when he stained the shirt, shot the bow, and sweated all over the heavy bag. It still feels heavenly inspired to give when we see an opportunity, and often in memory of our son and in honor of those who have given so lavishly to us. Generosity stirs generosity.

Kindness looks like showing up for someone else and with someone else in mind, just like loving the one in front of me. Those who showed up so graciously for us have further taught me through their example to follow my heart, not my head, as I think of someone. Seems that my head doesn't always interpret my heart well. As I go through my day and I remember someone that went Home early—or not—as estimated by human standards, I reach out to their loved ones to let them know that I remember...that I remember that they love and miss someone very important even if they only had each other on Earth for a short time. I try to say their loved ones name out loud and in current context. Acknowledging their loved one's birthday and the days when everything changed. Allowing myself to be changed by the people around me, by their lives and losses, is the least I can do to honor the gift of life.

I am more aware of the uncertainty of tomorrow, or the next 5 minutes for that matter. As a result, I am doing my best to love the one in front of me more consciously. I am working on sticking up for someone who's being mistreated, feeding people, sharing my stuff, lending my strength, giving money, holding the door, and saying *bless you* after someone sneezes. I am choosing to smile more at strangers. Now, I hug people the first time I meet them and definitely, as we say goodbye, I am practicing being honest about how the person who's not earth-side anymore has impacted my life and my heart. It really takes guts to say some of the things that need to be said. Honoring loved ones is often the precious, perfect, life-giving blessing for the hearer. We all need to know that our loved ones still matter, that they are still precious and precious to us.

I've also learned to be patient with people who are hurting, even if they hurt for a long, long time, which is the work of saints, and I have known a few! Just as we had been invited when we were hurting/grieving/traumatized (shell-shocked also comes to mind), we are practicing inviting hurting people too, to dinner, to coffee, or wine, or to church, or out for a hike, hopefully finding ways to laugh and with the intention of listening well. Our friends, Mark, Leslie, Shannon, Jason, Doug, Barbara, and Ian, are just a few of them who have been especially good at asking questions and actively listening for the sake of listening. They've been so generous with their hearts, hugs, and compassionate listening.

I have found that choosing to be kind, even when it is a lot of work, will always be the golden answer. Even though it can require a ton of compassion and endurance, choosing to sow kindness like an investment literally looks like a deposit of goodness that can completely change someone's internal atmosphere. Kindness is powerful enough to completely alter how we experience a moment.

Even choosing kindness sacrificially while my heart is actively hurting shifts enough of my focus and energy that I can begin to feel hope bumping around in my heart again. Hope is the expectation of good. There's just something EXTRA heavenly in those moments where hope is fresh while kindness and hurt are upfront. Kindness as an investment costs us something, and kindness always pays exponentially.

Ripples of kindness last so much longer than the initial act/gift at the moment it was given. Even the memory of kindness is enough to stir those waters again.

Return to your stronghold, you prisoners of hope.
Even today, I declare that I will restore double to you.

—Zechariah 9:12

DOUBLE SPEAKS OF HEAVEN'S RESPONSE TO US AS WE **stay in hope**, and I want it! I want all of what Heaven is holding for me, and I need all of Heaven while I'm on Earth. I am ever anticipating what double restoration could possibly mean and what double looks like for us. Do you want double restoration, too?

What would that look like? It's OK to stay in hope. It's OK to want it, and it's OK to keep going and live again.

But as Tom Zuba writes, "**This.is.not.easy**."

(THE FOLLOWING "CHOOSE LIGHT" POEM IS FROM TOM Zuba's book, *Permission to Mourn.* His whole book has ministered to me.)[iii]

"Choose Light"

TOM ZUBA

There is nothing
nothing
easy about this thing called grief.
Nothing.
But I ask you to please
please
please
say yes
more than you say no.
Say yes to you.
To possibility.
To hope.
To love.
To life.
To healing.
Please choose the light
more often than you choose the darkness.
Not that there aren't gifts in the darkness.
But it's often so much easier to find them
the gifts
in the light.
Do all you can to stay in the light.
Please remember that the person you love

so

so

so dearly

Lived.

Don't forget that.

He lived.

She had a life.

Here with you.

And your relationship continues.

Always.

ALWAYS.

Always.

Try not to be so overwhelmed

and paralyzed

and pissed off

that he died

that you spend most of your time

focusing on her death.

Say yes as often as you can.

Choose light as often as you can.

Remember that he lived

as often as you can.

Don't lose her

in the details of her death.

This thing called grief is hard

hard

hard work.

But you are stronger than you think.

You have already walked through fire.

And you can do it again

and again

and again.

To live well, we need to grieve well; we need to grieve completely.

Completeness is the presence of pain in the separation caused by the loss of our loved ones and the joy that can somehow be present simultaneously. Recognizing the joy doesn't diminish the significance of our loss or pain. It's just coexisting. Learning to live on one foot *here* and one foot *there* can be exhausting and exhilarating.

I remember feeling utterly shell-shocked and bewildered while strangely peaceful our first week home without Gian. I would "forget" and then suddenly "remember" with what felt like a violent and nauseating slam to my physical self and to my mind. Adjusting seemed a daunting and impossible task. How were we supposed to get used to this unnatural new normal?

Just as God's grace had been present on the day Gian was born, God's grace would continue to hold us together and bring to us the encouragement we would need to hold on, to keep breathing, to feel free to smile while crying, and to bravely go to sleep and let a new day happen.

God's grace would bring messages of truth, peace, and strength, messages of Gian's reality that would impact our present by helping us see into eternity.

Finding the Gold

Have you been crushed by a wave, too? What does your wave include? Does your wave involve living apart from someone you love very much? What is their name? Is your wave a different kind of experience altogether? Describe your wave and how you are coping and staying engaged in life.

....

....

....

....

....

....

....

....

....

....

....

....

....

....

....

....

....

....

....

....

....

....

....

We have a promise, and you and I both have it. Those who sow in tears WILL reap in joy! (Psalm 126:5). *That's a bold one...all that I've lost as evidenced through my tears, will be returned to me expansively. Have you begun to recognize joy in the midst of the pain? Are you open to joy?*

....

....

....

....

....

....

....

....

....

....

....

....

....

....

....

....

....

....

....

....

....

....

....

....

....

....

....

....

THREE

Anne's Prayer

WE BELONG TO EACH OTHER

Tell your heart to beat again.
~ Herms, Phillips, & West

Anne is a dear friend from years ago; she and I hadn't been in regular contact for quite some time...and I am still so honored by how God erases things like time and space as boundaries or limits to our love for one another, and just how deeply our love (whether we know it or not) for one another runs. We are far more connected than I've understood.

Tragic losses on Earth are understood differently, completely in Heaven. What is honored in Heaven is commonly misunderstood here on Earth. When a person dies having lived with Heaven in mind, onlookers could view that with criticism or confusion. I certainly have. Now, I understand that our loved ones' lives and their loss actually paved the way to a breakthrough.

Dear Alanna,

This was so difficult to write out. I originally just wrote about the prayer vision but found it didn't really make sense without going into my own faith battle. Still, it felt like it was about me, which I didn't want. At any rate, I've prayed over this and hope that my clumsy writing doesn't take away from the treasure hunt you are on.

Essentially, it starts like this. There is a beloved in my own family who has a diagnosis I'm not at liberty to share (it's not my information), but they will face a lifelong challenge because of this extremely rare genetic mutation. It's not even a matter of "healing'. It would require transformation at the genetic level. This... messed me up. And frankly, I was... angry. Really, really, really angry.

A lot of other things were going on in the church around the same time. Too many things. Our church imploding. Families were leaving left and right. Elders walking off. I was so bewildered. Every sermon and every teaching seemed to be a personal indictment and condemnation, and I couldn't understand any of it. I felt so lost...and just couldn't seem to find my way back. I didn't know where God was in all of this... and I couldn't hear Him.

Well, it went something like that. For quite some time.

Then, I learned of the crash from a posting on f/b. Another DAMNABLE thing I couldn't understand. That Sunday, Madison shared some details about the crash before church in the little home where we were meeting. Pastor taught first, and once church was over, we prayed for Gian. Pastor had asked something like, "What do we need to pray for?" Madison answered, "That Gian live and not die." Somehow, in all the hell-borne noise and turmoil and confusion I had labored under for about a year, during this prayer, in this moment, something shifted. The anger drained away, and I was... broken. Heartsick over everything I was seeing. Please, God, help me understand. And while I called out to God, I saw this while we were praying for Gian:

Your son was in a hospital bed. All along one side, there were people praying but it was more than just the people who were physically in the room. It was every person who was praying. Every single prayer was there in that room, shimmering at the edges and lifting to Heaven. I was aware of the earnest, love-drenched ache of each and every whispered plea from hundreds of hearts ...and so was Gian. But Gian was looking into the light, Alanna, gazing steadily into the pure glow on the other side. I could only see the edge of it, but Gian could look through it. I whispered, "Gian, just turn your head." And I meant, toward those praying. Toward this world and life here. But he kept gazing into the light, toward his Lord. Gian could see Heaven. And somehow, I knew that's what I needed to do. To stop looking at everything around me and keep my eyes on the Author and Finisher of my faith.

Then I heard a still small voice, "It is finished" and that's when my prayer vision ended and suddenly there was no more prayer within me.

When everyone else stopped praying, I left. I drove to the grocery store, stopped in the parking lot, and checked my phone and that's when I saw....

I visited you a few days later – I don't remember exactly what day. I doubt you remember due to the shock and grief – that crushing heart-smash. I wanted so desperately to do something, anything. I messaged a few times offering to pick up things you might need. People forget about the everyday things like toilet paper and you said I could pick up some TP for you. You were probably just sick of me offering, and remembering now that I was the bearer of toilet paper in that hour of need seems kind of funny, in a bitter-sweet way. On the way to your home, I felt a sense that I should tell you about the prayer vision but I talked myself out of it. I'm not sure I had faith that it was real... or would be helpful. At any rate, beautiful, overwhelmed, gracious you welcomed me and told me about the crash. About his best friend's grandfather intubating him. The airlift. Other heart-breaking details that you must have been absolutely sick from having to think about. You said you knew you could pray him back...but you gave him the choice. You told me people might not agree, but you know you did the right thing. You told me you asked him – and even though medically, it should not have been possible, and Gian shook his head. And I KNEW, Alanna, that Gian heard every whispered prayer of love. I KNEW that Gian shook his head even though it wasn't medically possible, and I KNEW, Alanna, that the prayer vision I had seen was from God. And I desperately wished at that moment that I had had the faith in God to believe what he showed me and the courage to tell you what I had seen in the prayer vision before you told me all these things. Because I believe that would have been confirmation for you, just as what you told me was confirmation of what God had shown me. And it wasn't that Gian chose not to stay, Alanna. Gian was looking into Heaven - Perhaps so heavenly-minded that stepping over into that place was so easy to do. Such puny, infinitesimally small comfort when you so desperately desire that he be HERE, but I think perhaps it can be both things at the same time. The heartache of his absence...and the comfort that he is with Jesus and you will see him again.

I'm not any closer to understanding why this happened. I didn't understand then, and I don't understand to this day. Nothing will ever make sense in the theft of your beautiful son or in the diagnosis I wrote of earlier. Somehow, though, for me, the "why" no longer matters as much since I stopped looking at the events and instead have turned to watch and listen and trust that somehow my Lord and Savior will make good of all of this. And I've come to understand the test isn't what we go through, and none of that garbage is from God. There's a hate-ful, hate-filled enemy that is doing everything he can to separate us from the one true God who loves us. The temptation is to abandon God. Our only hope and salvation, though, is God - in the midst of it. In spite of it. I understand Job better now. He was lost and crushed, beset and overcome, bewildered and angry - but he still looked to his God. That's why God showed me that prayer vision. Gian was looking unto his Lord and Savior... and that's what Gian showed me to do in the midst of my battle.

"I have told you all this so that you may have peace in me. Here on Earth, you will have many trials and sorrows. But take heart because I have overcome the world." John 16:33

With all my heart, I hope this somehow adds to your treasure.

Much love, Anne

We don't always get what we want in the way we want it. There are natural transactions on Earth that will leave us wondering till we're in Heaven together.

From my Facebook post, December 8th, 2017

Clarity on the 8th of the 25th month.

I completely misunderstood...of course! How could I possibly plot any kind of course for the unfathomable? Much less have any semblance of a clue. I thought leaving Harborview without Gian was the end.

I see a different reality now.

Those first steps were simply the beginning. Heartsmash obliterated every bit of casual lifestyle, ideology, and theology in me...oh boy. Talk about undone. The pieces of me have had to be reassembled with a Heavenly fixative. In some ways, unrecognizably so. Grace is the fixative, for sure. And FAVOR.

Just as the gift of my baby boy was surely evidence of Heaven's favor toward me, that same gift returned to his Giver. That boy, that favor wrapped up in the firstborn, is still mine. The favor that entered my life, our family, and our community continues. Partially on my demand, mostly by nature of the favor itself, and the favor of the Giver.[i] *I'll only be satisfied when we're together again; until then, I simply require more evidence of good, more of Heaven than ever. Anticipating my tackle at Heaven's gates and yet seeing, feeling, and recognizing an increase of goodness since G left for Home. Favor multiplied.*

THE SONG "ALL THAT LIVES FOREVER" BY STEFFANY Gretzinger is worth a listen. I've had it on repeat several times since hearing it for the first time. Her lyrics are a kind, gentle reminder that even stars fade and fall from the sky, but love is all that lives forever.

Gian's love for those around him, our love for him, and the way our loved ones chose to respond during this time resounded the love of God in unimaginable ways.

Curiously, as favor multiplied, so did the opportunity to defend our hearts as our deep-dive experience into traumatic loss heightened. An expectation from the outside began to emerge as our suffering became clearer and longer lasting than some preferred to witness.

Finding the Gold

Anne's vision helped me and still helps me to stay engaged in the mysterious parts of life, as I certainly don't understand much of what happens on the planet. And yet, in life, there is often comfort and companionship along with devastation.

How has Heaven met you here and in the mysteries present in your own life? Has comfort come through the presence of another person? A dream? Tell me.

FOUR

Posture Of Forgiveness

RELEASING TO JUSTICE & TO THE LOVE OF GOD

My ashes will be my boast.
I am becoming more beautiful.
Beauty is being added to me wholly.
~ Anonymous

To have a posture of forgiveness requires an introduction of its own. Forgiveness is not the same as saying it's OK, or I'm OK, or what happened didn't hurt, or that what happened wasn't a big deal.

Forgiveness means that I have, as an act of my will--not my emotions or the simplicity of it--released the responsible driver to justice and to the love of God. Yes, I have released her to both. I want zero responsibility for interfering in her process, or in my own for that matter. God knows my incredibly human heart perfectly and completely, and He's helping me to have a hands-off posture in my thought and prayer life towards her. She is God's business, not mine.

My forgiveness has come with a massive price tag, one that I didn't choose and one I ***get*** to keep paying.

Jeff and I have used the analogy of losing a leg to try to describe what our family has endured. Imagine if it had only been my right leg severed in that crash. The absence of my right leg would be evidence that I have survived something that my leg did not and that I have experienced a life-altering event and am missing part of myself as a result. In our case, this came about as a result of someone else's choices. That part is significant.

Legally speaking, the monetary value of a limb is over a million dollars. One might conclude that a son would be priceless.

Daily life without my right leg would change EVERYTHING. Getting out of bed, getting ready for work, taking our puppy out to potty, moving around our home, climbing stairs, or giving a hug —life without my right leg would affect every part of everything for me. Goodness, how about the empty pant leg? What about the ongoing physical pain of the event itself, of how my body is responding to the original injury, to the daily acclimation? What about the ghost nerve sensations? How would a missing leg affect my ability to hula hoop or dance? What about pushing a shopping cart? Driving? Walking? The addition of a prosthetic leg could be helpful in many ways, but would my gate ever be the same?

Would forgiveness result in my forgetting that my right leg was abruptly removed from me? Is forgetting considered a healthy outcome of forgiveness? What exactly would be forgotten? Would forgiveness result in the miraculous return of my right leg? Quite possibly, but that is not within my control. Would forgiveness make any part of my daily life less challenging? Less physically painful? Less emotionally painful? Maybe. What about necessary personal or societal changes? How do those take place if we forget?

I am reminded of a precious opportunity I was given to pray for a wonderful young man who needed healing in his body. There was a time when Jesus healed every shoulder I prayed for. He loves to heal what is hurting.

This young man was an active, engaged husband with hopes of becoming a father. At that time, his injury was impacting him in such a way that he was nervous to have children because he didn't know if he would be able to carry them, much less play with them. He was in a lot of daily pain despite medical care and intervention.

He so graciously allowed me to pray for him, although he had been prayed for many times before with no change that he could feel.

> *As we began,* ***I saw*** *a white bird with silver-tipped wings fly across the room. As I watched the bird, I heard the words, "Healing rides on the wings of forgiveness."*

There wasn't a physical bird in the building. Holy Spirit allowed me to see and hear what He knew needed to happen for His beautiful son to be free of the pain.

I shared what I saw and heard with the young man and his wife and proceeded to invite him to forgive the person responsible for his injuries. He had already forgiven her, and yet this was an opportunity to come into agreement in another way. His words seemed to get caught in his mouth as he attempted to form them himself, so I offered to lead him in prayer and for him to simply repeat after me if he felt like the words were true to him. So he did. When we were done praying, he exclaimed that not only was his shoulder completely free of pain and that he suddenly had full movement, but that his entire arm was no longer atrophied! I had no idea his whole arm was impacted! Forgiveness can be the key to unlocking the healing, restoration, and redemption we need.

This next portion stirs a TON of memories, anger, and gratitude. Anger directly related to the fact that what could have been prevented wasn't. Anger over being required to defend Gian's value as a human being in a legal setting, when my whole life I (blindly) trusted those in authority over me, socially, legally, and politically. I assumed that everyone around me, generally speaking, was choosing to "treat others as they wanted to be treated,"[i] especially other mothers. Anger in connection to every single thing that rubbed up against my smashed and very tender offended heart.

Especially in the first three years, nearly everything rubbed up against my heart. Oh man, was my heart, my mind, and my soul ever smashed (think banana in the hands of a toddler) and incredibly OFFENDED, like in a super fiery way. Imagine a red-hot fireplace poker shoved into your chest cavity and left to dangle there. Strangely enough, gratitude and laughter would buoy the sinking effects of heartsmash (as I used to say). More on that later.

In addition to acclimating to life apart from Gian, the first two years were drenched in devastatingly ugly legal details that did absolutely nothing to help our heartsmash, and these details seemed to arrive at least every two weeks as if on some kind of sadistic schedule. While I probably sound ungrateful to have been informed of the legal development, the gut-punching reality is I desperately still wanted to be included in everything related to Gian. Horrifying or not.

There were days that I thought, "OK. This is it. This is where I drop dead." I did not understand how my heart could keep beating, and I did not believe that I could handle one more filthy detail pertaining to the crash. Dropping dead seemed possible and likely. Now that I am on the outside of the legal *stuff*, I look back at those years and can see that the grace of God was literally holding us together. I completely understand why marriages and families implode, explode, or simply dissolve. I get why loved ones get sick, die early, lose their minds, and give up on life. I get why people turn to drugs, alcohol, food, and/or working too much (I have experience with some of that myself), anything to escape, to cope, to dull the very intense and searing pain, or just feel something different. The physical, emotional, and mental anguish we endured was nothing I have words for. Some of you get that. The lead Prosecutor of the case used the word *bleak* to describe our human experience without an attempt for a response, for an attempt at justice.

Burying my face in Love became my place of survival, refuge. I discovered I could only be completely honest with God, as He loved me, f-bombs and all. I knew that if I chose to be that transparent with my loved ones, I would only be smearing them with the acid in my heart, and I just couldn't hurt them any more than they already were. There was only **One** who could handle what I needed to say. During those first two years, many of my prayers boiled down to just two words: "Fu@%! Help!" I wasn't cussing at God, and this certainly isn't a prescription for prayer at all. Cussing hasn't been part of my vocabulary for a very long time, and yet my expression was coming from a place of intense pain. Like the time my hand was slammed in the car door, it was an expression of my pain, not my disrespect. At one point, following another horrid conversation with the attorneys, I found myself screaming, in a blood-curdling way and at the top of my lungs, in front of a nativity scene at a local Catholic church at Christmastime, no less. Yeah, I was that extra special lady. I have no idea if anyone was around or not. I just owe it to you, to be honest. And you need to know that when the only words I could form were "fu@%! Help!" Father God showed up so lovingly, so strongly, so kindly, and helped in those moments. He's not the religious one; we sometimes are, though. At my ugliest, He showed up, called me beautiful, and welcomed my honesty, snot, tears, lack of ladylike language, and all. I never felt shushed in my ugly, transparent heartsmash. As trauma began to work hard to take over our lives and incapacitate us, I only felt His "I know. I know. I love you." His heart is warm, safe, and kind.

As contradictory as it may seem, we laughed really hard too! We laughed probably just as hard as we cried, looking like completely crazy people, I'm sure. Joy really intervened in amazing ways and at just the right moments. Happiness and joy are distinctly different, as happiness is derived from circumstances, and joy is a gift from Heaven that is meant to sustain us. Joy is our strength for life,[ii] in all circumstances...and beautiful, incredibly strong friends, family, and even strangers showed up to brave the rough waters with us. Laughter, joy, silliness, and, strangely, gifts would arrive and interrupt some of the hardest moments. These interjections offered hope that not every moment of every day would be stacked so high with ugliness and pain.

We found ourselves thrown into a very steep learning curve, and typical to any emergency, there's a flurry of activity, a rush to stop the bleeding, to apply cold to a burn, throw water on the fire, assuming it's not an electrical fire...we definitely needed immediate care, but the care would prove to be an ongoing intensive labor of patience, not a onetime slap of a Band-Aid as our wound would not heal easily or quickly. The suffering made learning all the more challenging. We had never navigated life like this before.

Here is an example of what the *posture of forgiveness* looks like.

On the way to the emergency room that night, before Gian was life-flighted to Harborview in Seattle, WA, Jeff and I had no option but to weave our way through the five wrecked cars in the very same intersection just an hour or so after the crash, and as we did, forgiveness began pouring out of me. Out loud. Not unlike projectile vomit, actually, and even though I had no idea **what** or **why** or **who** I was forgiving. I literally could not keep it in, and as the events resulting from our last weekend with Gian were exposed, forgiveness would also be unleashed in a way that I had not yet experienced. I chose the word *unleashed* because my forgiveness behaves like an unrestrained and ferocious guard dog going after an intruder or a threat, chasing down, attacking, and subduing whoever, whatever, does not belong within my boundaries, within my heart. My forgiveness is growing, expanding, and becoming more precise, even more ferocious with each day away from Gian. Forgiveness is not a doormat, is not passive, and can be messy, expressing itself differently with each opportunity.

"I forgive you" is not the same as saying, "It's OK, or I am OK."

Forgiveness is releasing the person and entities that harmed us to the love and justice of God—while freeing ourselves from a death grip vice seeking recompense.

The sentencing of the responsible driver did not equate to justice for us.

The death grip vise I am thinking of is the one that thirsts for revenge, for payment, to be recompensed even by force, to work out *justice* in our own way, of our own design—a vigilante style of justice. Think of an "eye for an eye".[iii] There is a very real risk of getting too close to a baby bear. We all know this. Human mothers are potentially just as invested, just as motivated, just as responsive, and just as potentially destructive and ultimately deadly to any perceived or actual threat. I can assure you that if grace were not actively involved in my daily life and had not constrained me, I would be no different than the most average mother bear responding to the harm of her cub. Grace literally CONSTRAINS me, protecting everyone around me, and I am so grateful for it!

Originally, I thought I would title this portion "Accusations of Unforgiveness." This phrase came to me as I read a letter submitted by a gentleman (a personal friend of the responsible driver) to the local newspaper regarding the crash and wrote on the importance of forgiveness; he believed that she was also a victim. While the letter was eloquently written, it was completely out of place and written out of ignorance. He assumed we had not forgiven her.

When God forgives us, ALL is washed away. Everything is new. The record against us is erased. There's no debt to pay...as far as the east is from the west,[iv]is how far we are separated from our sins, although we may still have consequences for our actions. Consequences are a natural part of life and are important, especially when the things we do and the choices we make hurt those around us. Laws are created to ensure our behavior is aligned with group expectations so everyone can live safely; they are to protect and preserve our rights. Laws protect people, property, life, and rights. Laws are enforceable. For some of us, the enforcement of the laws or consequence piece is the only motivator for compliance or conscientious living. My neighbors can feel safe living next to me because I would never set their home on fire. I don't need a law to tell me that it's wrong or illegal to trespass and destroy another person's property. Some of us need the laws for a list of do's and don'ts, and so we have them. Forgiveness can occur on a personal, relational, or Supreme Court level. However, the Supreme Court of our state required her, the driver, to answer to the laws she broke that night. The roles of the Church and those of the governmental judicial system are distinctly different, and they are often confused.

Regardless of whether we forgive or not, the state laws were upheld. I didn't write the laws (they would be stronger if I had), nor was I responsible for her violating the laws. Based on the evidence and statements provided, it was important for her to answer to those violations in a court of law. As a grown woman practicing her free will, she created this situation for herself, her loved ones, and for us.

When someone is responsible for the death of your loved one or your child, you learn some things. You learn some really ugly and disgusting things actually about how the legal system works, or how it doesn't work, about society, and about yourself. Forgiveness was then and continues to be an active part of my life, AND justice is God's idea.

That's worth writing again. Justice is God's idea.

Justice is in the bible 328 times. Forgiveness is mentioned less than 200. I'm not arguing against forgiveness, attempting to undermine the significance of forgiveness, or trying to insert that justice trumps forgiveness, either. I'd never say that in a million years! I'm simply establishing that justice is **also** a topic with God. We are not wrong to thirst for it, as humans are wired for fairness and justice.

The idea of getting what we deserve or having natural consequences for our actions can make the toughest of us squirm. That's not what the justice system in Western cultures can provide anyway. We were warned against expecting any semblance of that in a Washington state court of law. Interesting, isn't it? Psalm 72:1

says it like this, "O God, make the king a godly judge like you and give the king's son the gift of justice too." I want justice for my son.

The justice I want for Gian will have to be far-reaching, life-changing. Confronting social norms isn't fun to me. I'd rather go with the flow and avoid drama, but I am compelled to push back on darkness by speaking the truth in love.

I've come to understand that some folks don't know what to do when they observe a soul on fire. Some have tried to extinguish the fire by devaluing the flames instead of letting the heat impact their own lives, instead of really feeling it, instead of looking at their own behavior, and instead of changing. What happened to Gian required an answer.

After some time sitting with "accusations of un-forgiveness," I have made a course correction. I am choosing to share this part of my creative and personal process because a wildly offensive scenario began to play and then replay as the days increased following the crash. Within just weeks, well-intentioned and completely innocent people (in addition to the newspaper contributor) who loved Gian, whom we also loved, suggested that we needed to forgive, that our ongoing and increasingly painful experience was tied to a lack of forgiveness. It is absolutely true that healing is tied to forgiveness, yet complicated grief/loss/trauma requires care and, unfortunately, patience. Forgiveness does not always equate to a painless existence. Losing Gian HURT. It still hurts. Someone actually said, "At some point, you have to move on." I don't recommend saying that, *ever*—to anyone. To witness the suffering that increases with time is alarming, no doubt. I've been alarmed myself.

These suggestions translated to us as: "You are responsible for your suffering. What happened to Gian is not important to us anymore. I am tired of your pain. You are a party pooper. Go fix yourself." Regardless of the validity of this translation, my soul heard these statements when they were said, **and we felt it**.

. . .

LOVE IS LONG-SUFFERING, AND SOMETIMES LOVE suffers a long time.[v]

Love *sees* those enduring loss and injustice with compassion, patience, tenderness, and love is driven to comfort and protect gaping raw wounds from further injury and exposure.

My definition of Heartsmash is:

- broken heartedness or
- the profound presence of permeating pain amidst wrangling forgiveness into the layers of devastation is evidence that "something" has happened, and
- "I am hurting because I have been hurt."

To those of you who have stayed the course with us and loved us through it all—you are our superheroes!

MANY YEARS AGO, I WAS WORKING IN THE KITCHEN, AND as I turned away from the counter, my elbow swung back and slammed into Gian's front teeth, knocking one of them out! He only gasped, but I screamed and apologized profusely, doing all I could do to comfort him, and tried unsuccessfully to get the baby tooth back in place. (Sometimes, teeth will reattach.) Anyway, even with my apology, and even though Gian forgave me, his face hurt, and he still lost a tooth! (Yes, the tooth fairy emptied out her pockets that night!)

Regardless of how inconvenient and awkward pain and suffering are, there are no quick fixes, fancy pills, magical prayers, wands to wave, drive-through options, or easy swaps for pain...I can say that I have been one of that crowd, assuming something must be wrong with the hurting because the hurt continued after my endurance or tolerance for their pain had dried up. I've behaved so badly on many occasions in this specific area, so I get it.

And to the man who wrote the letter to the newspaper and the others who haven't walked a mile in my shoes, as the saying goes, yet have still judged me as unforgiving because I continue to be impacted and because I have supported Ms. M. experiencing some consequences for her actions...**I forgive you for judging me, for misunderstanding what you've seen or heard.** I forgive you and release you to the love of God. AND, I am so grateful that they don't understand. Hopefully, they never, never will.

I have turned my focus to love and am determined to love people well enough for forgiveness (or any facet of healing and wholeness) to organically occur when it's time and in whatever form wholeness, forgiveness, and healing take. I have let go of attempting to control those outcomes for myself or anyone else, and I no longer assume that I would be privy to such a deep work happening within anyone else. Dealing with my own heart keeps me quite busy.

My own forgiveness has been continual, ugly, messy, generous, sharp, sometimes with strings attached, genuine, easy, calculated, liberal, spontaneous, aggravated, specific, broad sweeping, painful, joyful, holy, fruitful, a lot like breathing in and out, and worth it.

As long I am on the planet, I will undoubtedly remember and forgive and remember and forgive again. Every opportunity that has been taken from us with Gian will provide another opportunity to forgive.

Is there an option for a prosthetic son? Uh, no.

Every part of my being believes in and anticipates miracles. Miracles do happen and can follow forgiveness. I've seen that very thing happen with my own eyes, and wholeness is being fulfilled in accordance with Heaven's idea of redemption, which may be recompense. Heaven's version of wholeness is happening in us in response to our love, in response to what has happened to Gian, in our forgiving, and in response to God's own love for Gian and us. Father God's love for us is making us whole. Our healing is not a result of us attempting to make ourselves whole or denying the effects of life without the presence of our boy.

Heaven's justice is influencing our healing. Wholeness is so much different than I could have imagined. To date, wholeness would be joy-driven as deep down as my pain. Wholeness looks like maintaining boundaries of kindness, friendship, honesty, gentleness, and hope. Wholeness answers the question, "How many kids do you have?" with the answer, "I have 3 grown children."

Walking in forgiveness day in and day out means that I have released her (the woman responsible for the crash), even as I am continuing to be impacted by her. She cannot restore to me who she has taken from me. My forgiveness is not dependent on her apology (there's been none), her dedication to change, or any indication of ownership or responsibility in the events of the crash. My forgiveness is mine to manage—like my love—and my forgiveness is new for her every day. Though my forgiveness is more intentionally given when stirred by my heartsmash.

Forgiveness does not always result in a tidy, perfectly wrapped little package that is easy to handle and simple to give away. **Sometimes, forgiveness is so personally expensive, so deep, so continuous that it transpires like breathing or our heartbeats.** You don't get to witness it happening for someone else unless you are very, very close. What an honor to be so close.

Forgiveness is many "things," and it has become a holy, precision weapon of Heaven for me that I weald just as my heart aches for my son. Forgiveness reminds my heart of where to rest and where to trust. Forgiveness reminds me that justice originates with God and is fulfilled by God, as evidenced in the life of Jesus. He paid the full price, and I trust His intentions and His heart for Gian and me. His Love is fierce.

When I remind myself of the fierceness of the love that God allowed me to experience, forgiving continues to be possible because I need forgiveness, too.

. . .

Tony Evans once said, "Forgiveness is not pretending like it didn't happen or like it didn't hurt. That's called lying. Forgiveness is a decision to release a debt regardless of how you feel."[vi]

If I could, for a moment, wrap **precious you** in the arms of my heart in my love, I would...and I'd tell you, I'm sorry you've been hurt so badly.

I pray that as you have encountered my experience in this book so far, divine clarity will continue to do its work for you. Forgiveness is undoubtedly an act of our will that will need to be repeated day in and day out for you and me both, maybe for the rest of our lives.

Below is a prayer I have crafted with you and me in mind. Ultimately, when we forgive, we are also the ones who go free. If talking to God is new, or if being prayed for is new to you, it's as simple as, "God, I'm open, and I welcome the healing You have for me." Or, "God, I want to encounter You as my healer, as the Redeemer of my life." And then stay there. Don't wiggle away to business if stillness makes you uncomfortable. Ask the Holy Spirit, the Comforter, to help you stay and to keep returning until the work is completed and for as long as it takes, maybe for the rest of your life. You are worth it.

This is my prayer for you:

Father, first of all, thank You for the Gem reading these words and thank You that all limits of time, space, and distance are gone in the spirit realm, so You are with us both now.

Please pray this with me:

Father, please help us to walk in forgiveness from this moment forward, regardless of the mess we have been handed, how we and our loved ones have been treated, regardless of the ugliness we face, or the impossibility of the circumstances we currently sit in, regardless of the strength or authenticity of any apology or lack thereof.

Father, as an act of our wills, not as an act of our emotions, we forgive; we release all those who have trampled our rights and the rights of our loved ones. We forgive, we release all those that have offended Your heart and our hearts, as they have overstepped the boundaries of love and mistreated the apple of Your eye. As we forgive and release these people, entities, and organizations, we envision these jagged stones rolling out of our hearts and out of our open hands to land at Your feet for You to tend to. In Jesus' name, amen.

I highly encourage you to insert the specific names of those responsible for your hurt. Maybe you need to forgive yourself. Maybe you need to forgive God for allowing people to make their own choices. Pray out loud, and know that your prayers are heard and are being answered regardless of any feelings that follow or any recognizable change within you yet.

Your freedom from the weight of what happened to you isn't necessarily validated by feelings or a change in feelings. I'd like to invite you to rest and trust in the Creator of Heaven and Earth, and all that is in them, to take to Himself all that has come against you for justice to be worked on your behalf. He often waits for us to take our hands off.

The following was recently written by the youngest of our three. Our Zosia treasured and still treasures her beloved big brother. Both girls do. Witnessing them be robbed over and over again has fueled my forgiveness in still more ways.

"Zosia's Treasure"

ZOSIA

I got to watch my brother graduate High school in 2015. I never got a picture with him on graduation day... I regret that.

I got to see my brother get hired into the Naval Shipyard and hear how excited he was to be working in shop 56. I remember his steel-toed boots. The sound of him walking in the front door.

I remember him teaching me to drive his truck around our neighborhood when I was 14, the summer after he graduated. The summer before he was killed. The last summer I got to spend with my brother.

I am thankful to have spent 14 years with my brother. But I can't help but feel bitter that he only got 18 years. And here I am, at the age of 22. It feels wrong to have lived longer than my older brother had the opportunity to.

I am so thankful for the memories that I have of him. But I also hurt. Because those 14 years are all I have of him. Every milestone is bittersweet because he isn't there. He always made an effort to be there.

I'll never get to congratulate him on kicking off his career. I'll never see him buy the motorcycle he was planning on buying without my parents knowing. I'll never get to celebrate his engagement or his wedding. I'll never see his first home. I'll never see his children. I'll never see my brother past the age of 18.

I'll never be able to share my successes. I'll never be able to share my love, my job, what I learned that day. He wasn't able to be at my sister's wedding, and he won't be at mine. He'll never see my home. He'll never get to build a relationship with my future husband. He'll never get to meet my children. My children will never get to meet him. The family that I hope to have will only be familiar with his face from pictures and stories.

I will never receive older, brotherly advice from him again. I will never get to see him, hug him, or laugh with him again. He will never see his parents and younger sisters grow into the individuals that we are now. As much as we wish that he could be here so we could celebrate him... we also wish he could be here celebrating us.

I got to have my big brother by my side for 14 years. I wish he were still here. I wish I could see him turn 26 this year. I wonder what he would be like. Everyday, I am thankful for the memories I have. Everyday, I wish that we could've made more. What would life have been like if he were alive? Unfortunately, I'll never get to know.

DEATH, DESTRUCTION, ROBBERY, INSULT, INJURY, AND INJUSTICE WILL NOT BE HARBORED IN MY HEART.

I refuse to let the enemy[i] of life itself continue to have a say in my remaining days or to further rob me. I have determined to walk free and whole, increasingly so, and I turn over every foul weapon formed against me to the Champion of my soul.

Finding the Gold

Because love endures all things, and love never fails, describe what endurance is for you. (1 Corinthians 13). What are you enduring because you love? How does forgiveness impact your endurance? What is the price tag connected to forgiveness for you? For me, the price tag was control. Forgiveness included letting go of the idea that I would receive justice by holding on to the facts instead of trusting God to work it out for me. What does it look like for justice and forgiveness to hold hands in your own life?

....

....

....

....

....

....

....

....

....

....

....

....

....

....

....

....

....

....

....

....

FIVE

That Moment In My Unzipped Heart

HE IS GIVING ME BEAUTY FOR MY ASHES

Every single prayer was there
in that room, shimmering at
the edges and lifting to Heaven.
~ Anne, from Anne's Prayer

My heart has been camped out on wanting to reveal the goodness of God since November 6, 2015. I want my story to show Him as He, God, really is. I want to help dispel some of the harsh myths so many in the world believe to be true--some of the harsh myths that I had also believed. For instance, I believed that if I prayed the right prayers and did the right things, I could thwart devastation in every way, shape, and form. Having witnessed true miracles of healing in my own life, in my family members and friends, I just began to expect every prayer to be answered in the way I anticipated. Jesus didn't go around making people sick. He certainly didn't kill people's children...and then my dad needed more surgery, a cousin was killed in the Middle East, another cousin by drug overdose, our kids' friend at age 14 to accidental overdose, then my good friend's teenage daughter died in her sleep, then Gian's teammate's beloved brother was in an accident...and then Gian. And another boy, Gian's age, just 14 days later to a reckless/drunk driver. Then another teammate to drowning, and another to murder. Later, I found out that my good friend at work had delivered her second daughter, who was stillborn more than thirty years ago. Shortly after learning that, another coworker's son was shot and killed. So many beloveds to suicide both before and since COVID. Life (and death) had been happening all around me—us, actually. A dear friend who is battling cancer for the second time reminded me that we are all terminal. Like from the minute we're born, terminal. She and I have reframed that concept to recognize that **we are designed for eternity—from the minute we're born, we're born to eternity**.

The separation that death leaves in its wake is not part of our divine design. We weren't designed to be apart from our loved ones through death. Heaven's original plan did not include death, and that's why it hurts so much.

That moment in my unzipped heart occurred one early, early morning—probably in the 2nd year following the crash and around 2 am. This particular morning resembled so many others while Gian was still with us and, like many, many since he left. Yet, something unexpected and desperately needed occurred, something life-changing happened.

My alarm went off well before my family so that I could have time to prepare my heart and mind. My heart, although willing, would just sit painfully raw during the early mornings apart from Gian. The comfort I had knowing that he simply beat us Home (to Heaven) didn't diminish the pain of what occurred or our missing him. The promise of Heaven and a shared eternity provided **a certain endurance** to stay the course, though.

The back story to the early rising began when a very wise woman encouraged me to start getting up before my babies, before my husband, before the needs of the day were to be addressed, and often well before the sun. I was maybe twenty-three years old at that time. If you have cared for young children, you know how important it is to their wellbeing, for you to have your own needs met as well...so, for me, that meant I would set my alarm for two, sometimes three hours before they would wake to be ready for all the beautiful things that little tinies need. That habit stayed with me long after they weren't tiny anymore.

After the crash, these times would prove to be even more vital. Day in and day out, I didn't know if my heart would or even could keep beating much longer, and as my eyes opened each morning, I would roll my heart (all the issues of life originate in the heart)[i] out of bed and dedicate it and those times to the Lord acknowledging that apart from His grace, apart from His sustaining power there was nothing I could do to survive. **Not one thing**. I quickly learned that survival wasn't a matter of my will... I could feel my heart failing inside my chest. This was more confirming than scary to me. There were moments I acknowledged my desire to survive and potentially thrive again, but it only stirred because of our daughters. I would not add to their sorrow by giving up. I decided I would keep getting out of bed each morning to face our life, our devastation, our altered joy, and our stripped-naked hope. Being less than authentic would do none of us any favors, and I wanted to honor our girls by being transparent in my heartsmash. Their brother will always be worth my honesty. I love them too much to give them less than my whole heart.

Surviving what our son did not, combined with the legal aspect surrounding the crash, created an unspeakably painful moment-to-moment existence. The pain doesn't go away with time; however, I do believe we acclimate (sort of).

The moment I'm preparing to share with you occurred when the legal details of the event had been fully revealed and were actively playing out in the Court of Law. It felt to me that the legal responses were more focused on protecting the rights of Ms. M. and how her potential jail time would affect her own children rather than on how her choices robbed our son, Gian, of his life.

Of course, there is a legal response when laws are broken, when someone is responsible for the death of another person. The legal proceedings addressed that and were addressing her, but not necessarily the value of our son (although our souls literally screamed for it). I was invited by the Prosecution to hold the memory of Gian and the reality of her actions by addressing the Court or speaking directly to the Judge during two of the court dates, which was really painful, deeply satisfying, and an absolutely natural responsibility for me to accept. Like all the other important appointments and events in my children's lives, I was honored to be invited to participate. I never could have imagined the natural progression of motherhood would lead me to such an opportunity.

I had expected the laws of our land and the community we live in to prevent the preventable, to protect, and to defend our innocent son, his friends, and the people in the other three cars at that intersection. As the details became clear, we realized that our expectations were faulty, which added another layer of injury to our already massive loss. Truly, life is precious if ONLY in the eye of the beholder, AND yet always in the eyes of our Creator.

I hadn't considered the need for the innocent to be represented in order for the severity of the crime to be obvious.

Gian's girlfriend, Lawran, who was driving at the time, and her little brother, who was in the backseat, were not considered in the proceedings. In fact, they had to fight to be recognized by insurance providers as having suffered in the crash and as a result of Gian's death. They were in the same utterly demolished car, and it is a miracle they survived! These aspects further fueled my sense that the loss of innocent lives is valued only by insurance companies and our politicians when they benefit. My heart and mind were in turmoil.

This particular morning, I was sitting with the Lord on the floor, being thoroughly open with Him, and not knowing how to move forward with the day. I sat there crisscross applesauce on the living room floor with my eyes closed. In my mind, I held my devastated and exhausted heart in my hands, offering it to the Lord. Tears flowed like rivers down my face, soaking my shirt as I sobbed. I had no words, again, to offer the King of Kings. All I had was my battered heart and my presence to give. The throne of my heart and the honest tears would have to suffice this morning like they had countless mornings before and every foreseeable morning to come.

When suddenly, in my mind's eye, I **saw:**

> *The heart in my hands became like one of those plush educational toys that would unzip end to end and flay open to display the contents of the anatomy:*
>
> *Only in my plush heart there were flowers. A garden opened up in the heart resting in my hands.*
>
> *I felt puzzled and strangely peaceful as I gazed (in my mind's eye) at the garden full of unusual, stately flowers. These flowers were Technicolor™ vibrant, and the fragrance seemed to leak both their rich colors and perfume. The fragrance seemed to speak with words.*

I suddenly understood that the flowers were the garden of my heart. The garden with its flowers represented my truest self and how every detail of my truest self had been impacted by injustice, my unmet expectations, my unfulfilled hopes, my decimated dreams, my shattered sense of security, my simple trust of law, my community, my perceived failures as a mother and the life I was dedicated to living with my son and the devastation of my daughters as they chose to show up each day to try again without their big brother, their champion and my husband's heartbreak and rage over what had occurred and over the loss of our very good boy. The future we hoped for our family was in shards. Our future was always together. Incredibly, although impacted, each flower was still alive and stunningly beautiful.

As I sat there, my heart physically ached as I recalled Gian sharing how he wanted to live a strong, noble, and beautiful life. He gave of himself generously wherever he went. And he was living that at the time of the crash. He just wanted to work hard, be a good friend, earn his own money, and steward it well. He wanted to be an encouragement, a source of kindness and strength in the world.

He wanted to be married one day, and he wanted to be a father and an uncle...as I sat there with these flowers in their current reality, Jesus appeared:

> *Jesus so gently and thoughtfully stepped into the garden of my heart with His warmly radiant robes and slowly, slowly, began walking with His eyes, focusing on each flower with every step. Although I didn't see his eyes or even His face, I could feel His gaze. As He moved, His hands were ready, present with, and thoughtfully tended to each flower. Respect flowed from Him. Watching Him took my breath away. The colors and fragrances of the flowers were wet with my heartbreak and devastation, yet He did not shy away from the mess of any of them. As He walked, He recognized each one, acknowledging the enormity of what each had endured, taking His time with every bloom. Step by slow, intentional step, He paused with each one, truly encountering them with His kindness, thoroughly appreciating what they represented.*
>
> *At one point, I could feel myself pulling my heart back for fear that He would get messy and that the contents of my heart would smear or stain the Son of God. I feared that I would be too much for Him, but He just kept tending each flower. He was not distracted by my fear or my concerns. He was not intimidated or disapproving of my pain. The soppy wetness, the bleeding out of the flowers, seemed to reach for Him, and He seemed to be happy about their reaching. He responded to the reaching by turning His palms toward each one to receive and soothe them. He demonstrated such honor, tenderness, and care for each flower. He*

moved through my heart, slowly acknowledging all of it, every part, every detail related to the crash, before and after. His compassion was shocking at that moment, and I could feel His gentle smile and His joy over the contents of my heart. ***Hearts are His business.***

He held no surprise, no disgust, no disdain, or horror for me and my pain--none of that—only boundless tenderness for me, and humbling gratitude flowed from Him for being allowed into the garden of my heart. The fierceness of His devotion to me and to my son became evident as He allowed me to sense His own anger over how Gian had been treated. He wasn't OK with the crash either. He isn't OK with flippant responses to the lives of His children. He sees us all as His children. He assured me that justice originates with Him and that I desire it because He desired it first. He paid for our justice. He would surely work justice out for us, for our beautiful boy and his sisters. Not one tear is unseen. Not one tear is excessive. He has promised me that goodness would be chasing us down all the days of our lives as a direct result of our boy.

It was in that moment that I realized that He truly is near the brokenhearted.[ii] *Not that I have always felt Him near, because that hasn't been the case. Yet, at this moment, I recognized that He was right there, literally right in the midst of it, fully present, engaged, not disappointed, with no judgment, just a kind, kind knowing, and fierce love. He loves sons. He loves daughters.*

This encounter only lasted a few minutes, although time felt long and lavish. Then, it was over just as suddenly as it began. When I finally pulled myself off of the floor that morning, I recognized my heart felt secure, seen, understood, and deeply approved of. Safe. Held. I *felt* Father God's pride in my grieving, in my loving. **He has a Son, too**, and love is like that. Life is worthy of that. I felt permission to cry and laugh naturally and often simultaneously. I felt permission to hope and trust Him even in the mysteries as I continue to look to the Author of Life.

Some questions will not be answered on this side of Heaven, but we can invite Heaven to come and impact it all as we wait.

Just as I sat on my living room floor that morning, I'd like to encourage you to do the same. Set yourself up for an encounter with Christ the Healer. Maybe you already have created a time and space for your heart to be transparent, authentically unprotecting your cracked-wide-open heart, where you can be honest with yourself and Him about what is truly happening inside you, with what really happened, how you are impacted, and how you are coping. **Invite Jesus in**--like every, every, every day. **Invite Him into your mourning**. Invite Him to show you how He sees what has happened, what *is* happening, and the people involved. He will show you. Jesus **will show** how present He has always been.

Our awareness of His presence is a separate topic, but "Jesus step in" could be your invitation to the King of Kings and the Lord of Lords. He is all about hearts, and **He wants to care for yours**. He is completely trustworthy with our mysteries and devastations.

My heart cannot help but lean in—heartbeat by heartbeat—and choose to trust this "Man of sorrows."[iii] This is why He came. Jesus actually says that those who mourn are blessed because they will be comforted. He is the only One who can heal the broken-hearted.

> *To all who mourn in Israel, he will give a crown of beauty for ashes, a joyous blessing instead of mourning, festive praise instead of despair. In their righteousness, they will be like great oaks that the LORD has planted for His own Glory.*
>
> —Isaiah 61:3 *NLT*

That's a really big promise!

For beauty to be worked all the way through my ashes, and in order to recognize the gold, the Heavenly, in my ordinary moments, I need to be interrupted. I need my regular life stuff to get shaken up in order to appreciate how Heaven is present.

MEETINGS ON A STAIRWELL

One day, in year three, after the crash and while climbing a flight of stairs at work, I was suddenly and tangibly aware of Gian's presence next to me. Although I didn't see him with my natural eyes, I did *see* him, and I *felt* his presence.

> I looked past my left shoulder and said out loud, "Oh, you're bigger now!" and Gian replied, "I wasn't done growing."

And then he was gone.

That same week, I shared the story of a strange moment on the stairwell with Gian with my sister, and she told me about her Heavenly encounter with our Grama Gina. She had gone Home a few years before Gian. Annie shared that while climbing a stairway near the train tracks in San Clement, California, she suddenly caught the aroma of Grama Gina's perfume. She and I don't know anyone else who wears Grama Gina's perfume. No one else was there; she was entirely alone, but she felt comforted by the pleasant aroma of Grama's fragrance.

I believe these experiences are meant to show us that our loved ones continue beyond our sight. **Love is the force that connects us regardless of where we live.**

Life on earth is not the sum of life. Someday, we'll know what these unusual moments are really about in full, and for now, I am grateful that our loved ones have felt close at times and that our love for each other continues to impact and transform us. There are really no ordinary moments, and I am especially grateful for the ones that draw me Heavenward.

Finding the Gold

What does Motherhood or Fatherhood look like for you, and where has it brought you? What is being highlighted or sharpened in your own thought/heart life? Are you willing to do the brave, childlike work of embracing mystery to allow yourself to stay curious and observant, even expectant? What would it look like for more of that in your life?

SIX

Transformative Love

INTENTIONALLY LIVING TOWARD LEGACY

Some questions will not be answered on this side of heaven, but we can invite Heaven to come and impact it all as we wait.
~ Alanna

My mother's mother, Grama Gina, came to visit, hoping to be present for Gian's birth. My mom was her first baby, and I was her first grandchild, and he was her first great-grandchild and my parents' first grandbaby. Just days before G's birth, Grama Gina asked how I was feeling about our baby boy's impending arrival, and I confessed that I wasn't sure. I hoped we would like each other and that I would be a good mom to him. Mostly, I just remember feeling nervous and incredibly puffy!

Grama's wise response remains with me today. She said, "Don't worry; they bring their love with them."

Was she ever right. Just a few days later, and a full two weeks past his due date, I met Gian, my first true love. His Dadio (as Gian called him) and I would never be the same.

Gian's labor and delivery were rough for both of us. I'm sure he was hurting just as much as I was. He cried long and hard as the doctor and RNs completed his first exam until his Dadio leaned in close to speak comforting words into his fresh ears. I watched in amazement as Gian turned his head, locked eyes with his Dad, and fell silent. **Love at first whisper.**

I had no idea that this kind of love existed, and I was shocked that I was capable of it. Yet, I suddenly understood that this love was now somehow intertwining with my tiny boy's life, his flourishing, his voice, my breath, and heartbeat to his. While I could put myself in a memory of my life before Gian was born, I found it impossible to remember a time in my life apart from my love for him, and suddenly, I understood that my own life would never be independent of his, ever. Thoroughly, completely, and irreversibly in love. How could my heart be so completely and utterly wrapped around someone brand new to me? He couldn't do anything for me but make demands of my sleep, energy, and my body, and somehow that was perfect. His beauty alarmed me. How did I deserve such a beautiful gift? Clearly, I did not. I wondered how on Earth I could do him any good or be good enough for him.

So, his Dadio and I set out to learn the business of raising a prince.

Our young prince would become a big brother twice, and I have thoroughly enjoyed witnessing our children choose to become friends.

It has been my deepest honor to be their mother. To be Gian's Momma and his sisters' Mom, Mama, and Mommy. I've loved it all and worn the name tag each of my babies has given me through the years with great joy and pride. I'm so proud of my three Gems. My greatest work in life has been motherhood.

Our young prince was actively learning to navigate the challenges and adventures of life. By navigate, I mean recognizing the opportunity and obstacle and responding versus reacting or course-correcting with the destination or goal in mind. I am not insinuating perfection. If you know us, you know that perfection is actually not a thing we've aspired to. Not at all, only recognition of an upward call to life and a recognizable leaning into God's truth, love, honesty, generosity, kindness, humor, friendship, and faith. He was really trying, ever focused on finding the gold in the people around him. I am so proud of how Gian chose to live, and in my opinion, his work here wasn't done, but in 2014, he shared hints that he *knew*.

One day, as I passed through his bedroom, he turned to me and said, "I know I'm gonna take their grenade for some people."

As you might imagine, I was really caught off guard by that statement. And so I asked him, "What do you mean?"

He said, "I know I'm going to lay down my life for some people. There's no greater love than to lay down your life for one's friends."[i] While he wasn't wrong, I, like probably most other mothers in the world, was completely horrified and desperately wanted to press delete on what he had just said. His words terrified me. His self-sacrificing nature already made me uncomfortable.

And I chose not to live in fear. He belonged to God first, and I chose to trust Gian's life to his Abba Father, as he called Him.

Seven years later, and in accordance with our good God's perfect timing, just when another bit of gold was ready, a dear friend reached out and shared,

> *As I sat in the presence of the Lord, the Lord took me to that day of Gian's homecoming and showed me what actually happened in the spirit realm. I saw the Lord Himself come to Gian in those eternal seconds where time seemed to stand still and spoke to him before the impact of the cars. He let Gian know that many people could die as a result of this crash. When Gian heard that, he spoke up and asked that he be allowed to take the full impact on his body alone so that his friends and others might be spared.*
>
> *Jesus was blessed by Gian's willingness to stand in the gap on*

behalf of others. In response to Gian's act of compassion, the Lord mercifully removed his spirit being from his body before impact. I saw him leave with his guardian angels on either side of him with a huge smile. Gian was so happy! I was so impressed by Gian's words to you that he would one day lay down his life for others. This he most assuredly did!

John 15:13 Greater love has no man than this that a man lay down his life for his friends.

Love and hugs to you, my friend. M.

He and I often talked about ways that he could sacrifice, the ways he could **choose a life of significance**, even in the normalcy of his daily routine. He could sacrifice by really showing up well despite his own feelings and choosing to see people who needed to be seen. He could choose to **look for the gold in people** rather than focusing long on the dirt and choose to highlight that by encouraging the hearts around him.

We would talk about the ways that he could lend his presence and his strength, moment to moment. He would share his lunch with a hungry person. If someone was sad, he found out why and tried to be comforting. If someone was being bullied, he got in the way of that. He saw injustice and intervened; when someone needed a friend, he was a friend. If someone needed a place to rest, give them a place to rest. He emptied his pockets over and over. After the crash, we began to hear just how much he was doing that and how **he was intentionally living toward legacy**. Given his nature, we aren't surprised at all that he was, somehow and quite miraculously, the only one *hurt* in all five cars despite how damaged all of them were. I have absolutely no idea how that could ever be possible. Except that God loves Gian enough to make his life and his death deeply impactful. Making the very most of both. I believe God honored Gian even in his death.

There are natural transactions on Earth that we will wonder about till Heaven.

Before the summer of his junior year, he and a bunch of friends went to the drive-in. While they were waiting for the movie to begin, they heard screeching and then heard sounds of vehicles colliding. I remember he shared how he instantly jumped up and ran as fast as he could to the two-lane highway entrance of the lot, where he encountered a downed motorcycle and a truck. Two motorcyclists were thrown from their bikes and looked to be in bad shape. Fortunately, he had studied and participated in sports medicine for a few years in high school and had been trained in emergency care. Gian was able to assist as additional RNs and doctors who passed the crash also came to aid the injured motorcyclists. He was the first on the scene, actually. He later told me there wasn't anywhere else he would have rather been. From the time he was little, he would get closer to those that needed help. I love that about him. A couple years later, I met one of the nurses who was at the same scene. She actually met Gian and was able to tell me the same story after he had already gone Home. She was impressed by the calmness and focused care he was able to provide, especially for someone so young.

The phrase, "We only come this way once,"[ii] helps me to consider how I'm impacting, maybe even transforming, the world around me and possibly creating the final impression I'll leave people with. It boils down to today in how I treat my loved ones and coworkers, the folks at the grocery store and all the way to my Homegoing, whenever that is. Our impact, the legacy we are building, is being clarified and solidified even right now, in the next five minutes, and over the next fifty years. I've begun to ask myself, "What is the impact I want to have on those around me?"

How about you? What is the impact you want to have on the world around you?

What do you want your legacy to be? How do we want to impact those we intentionally interact with and those we have no idea we're affecting until we're gone. Gian wanted to be the goodness of God for people. He wanted to love people in the way they needed to be loved. He wanted to give in a way that would meet their truest need. He wanted to show up well for the world around him. And I think about how the woman who caused the crash has impacted me, even though I'm sure that wasn't her intention.

I am reminded of a time, several years before the crash while driving home, a question dropped into my heart. Sometimes, God gets my attention this way. A conversation started with a question, which unfolded question by question as I sat with the voice of the One asking:

"Would you trade your son?"

An image of a single anonymous person flashed in my mind. The question stunned me—horrified me. Even though I recognized the Voice, I was so caught off guard by the abrupt intensity of the question. I answered, "You know my heart, Lord. No, I would not trade my son."

He asked, "Would you trade your son for a household?"

"No, Lord."

"Would you trade your son for a neighborhood?"

"Lord, no, I wouldn't," and as I sat with what the Lord was unfolding in my heart, He gave me a picture of a city with the nudge of the same question.

My answer remained unchanged. I knew He wasn't threatening or challenging me. He wanted to reveal something.

The image in my mind's eye increased to include our state. Again, my heart aching, and my answer was still no. Then, He showed me the image of an entire country with the same question. "No. An entire country for the life of my son would still be too small. I would never allow it."

I was just being honest.

The image panned out to the view of the Earth from space.

I wanted to be able to say, "Yes, Lord. I would trade my son for the entire world," but my answer was firmly unchanged. "You know me! No one and nothing would be able to stop me from attempting to protect my son, even for the sake of everyone on the planet. I would never be willing! He is far too precious to me. And even if, for just a second, my heart could somehow agree to it, my body would then respond, and I would be separated from my limbs in order to escape any restraints preventing me from rescuing him. I'd use myself as a shield to protect him!"

I felt His satisfaction, His affection, even His smile in my reply. He then showed me every generation before me and every generation after me.

That's when I got it.

Father God would never be satisfied with the sacrifice of His Son's life until every single person in every single generation is swooped up in that trade and swooped up in His love. Every single one of us is an extremely precious part of Jesus getting His full reward, and God Himself will not be satisfied until His Son's beautiful life and sacrifice—the trade He made for all of us—is completed. Only then will He have His full Glory. Only then will the scales be balanced in the eyes of Love. God's love for His Son in exchange for us is not casual, flippant, or an easily satisfied love. His love is intensely accurate and constantly on the watch. My own love for my son is a very small representation of His.

That statement from Gian's nurse, "I have never witnessed such love before," still rings in my ears. I pray the love she witnessed has remained with her. All we had done was love him. The way we had all along.

Desperately, I crave the very greatest GOOD coming from the extremity of our loss as my love for him remains alive and well. The good coming has got to be enormous, boundless, overwhelming, and not just for me. For good to overwhelm our loss, the boundaries of *good* would have to be unreachable, flooding the lives of our loved ones and those of complete strangers. My version of good would have to be so big, so saturating, that every facet of our lives would be thoroughly slathered, drenched, even marinated in goodness. We have experienced some of this goodness, but by no means have we been satisfied with our need for it. We are waiting, watching, and expecting.

As I write (in the seventh year since the crash), I recognize my eagerness to see him, to hear him, to be with him again. My face remembers the feel of Gian's neck. My lips remember the texture of Gian's temples. I never knew lips could have a memory. His skin is like no other. I recognize my hope that he will just show up one day with his dirty boots on, rush over, and scoop me up in his arms to squeeze me. It's been a little too long since our last hug, and I wonder if hugs are as important, as life-changing things in Heaven as they are here.

I know Gian is still alive, *just beyond my natural sight.*

Love is like that. Regardless of where Gian lives, my heart is still completely invested in his thriving and enthralled by his voice, his laugh, his energy, his ideas, his silliness, his dirty socks, and his contribution to the conversation and the way he solved problems. I am forever his momma. I realize the implication of this kind of love, this kind of connectedness, that it suggests something devastatingly risky. True.

Love is like that.

We love him today just as much as the day he was born and just as much as the day his heart stopped beating at nearly eighteen and a half years old. He is just as wanted. Just as needed. His place with us is just as secure. His presence will not be filled by anyone else. Our hearts are, somehow, miraculously enlarged to welcome, with open arms, those that come our way. That vacuum created by G's Homegoing has seemed to bring every bit of goodness specific to his life, created by him and his choices, the goodness that was held in place by his presence in this life, the goodness due him, to us, since the place holder of his physical self was removed. We are scooping all of that gold up and keeping it as treasure, and yet our treasure is in Heaven.

That strange encounter with the questions provided the assurance I would later need. Had I not been convinced of God's incredible, rich love for Gian and for our daughters, I probably would have lost my mind as the details of the crash were revealed and as legal actions began.

I would bury my face in the love of God. That same fiery, justice-loving heart would become my place of refuge to survive what felt like the fight of my life to defend Gian's value as a human being, as a son, as a brother, as a cousin, and as a friend.

Years ago, I was introduced to the statement, "Just love the one in front of you."[iii] Jesus actually said it right to me while I was on a walk and feeling super confused about some pretty big things, especially about the role of the Church in my life. And that's what He said. Sounds simple, doesn't it? It is so simple until fear or hurt, confusion, harm, injustice, or death tries to enter. I have been tempted to go gun-shy with my love. But instead, I've allowed myself to become an awkwardly long hugger, and I say "I love you" often and repeatedly. I find myself really, really soaking in moments with our daughters. Like, really soaking them in. Just like when they were babies, I've gone back to studying their smiles and the color and shape of their eyes. While our girls are grown now, I'm thirsty for their presence and recognizing that each of them continues to evolve right before me and in the moments that I look away, even for a second. Time is precious, and the whole point of time is to navigate life to be with our loved ones...in my opinion, and to directly challenge my gun-shy temptation, I have become more vocal about my love for my friends and family, recognizing I might only have right now to tell them how precious they are to me, so I do. I want my loved ones to be convinced of my love. I want zero guessing about that. Actually, I want strangers to feel it, too. If people could be healed by Paul's shadow,[iv] I want my shadow to reveal the love of God. Although I feel nervous sometimes that my love for people won't be understood or won't be reciprocated, and sometimes it's not, my love is mine to give. And I need to give it.

I'm not talking about romantic love or the love I have for cheese, and especially for chocolate cake and peanut butter. I'm talking about the kind of love that takes a bullet for a stranger or enters a burning building to save somebody else's family, the kind of love that makes it completely natural for parents to stay up all night to comfort their sick child when they have to leave for work early in the morning...the same kind of love that drove Jesus to the cross and compelled Him to stay on it until it was finished.[v,vi]

That kind of love.

Love creates for us, and loss/mourning/grief born out of love can present an opportunity for love (or fear), for the expansion (or shrinking, think shriveled like beef jerky) of our hearts, and for goodness (or bitterness) to enter our lives.

The risks associated with staying tender to love challenge me, but guarding my heart from potential devastation again means that I'll end up keeping everyone at a safe but chilly distance--and where is the good in that? My arms keep searching for a young man that feels like mine to squeeze. While I've hugged dozens of them, and they've all felt like wonderful sons, warm, smelling like dusty sunshine...they just aren't my boy. My arms know the difference. So, I hug them anyway, choosing to soak in the goodness and beauty held in the hug of someone else's son. I am so grateful for other people's sons. In the last handful of years, I've met several who have needed or missed a mom's hug. If that's all I have to offer the world going forward, I might be just fine with that.

If we turn our love or our hearts off toward the world and the people around us, we run the risk of missing the wholeness of the good that can come. I don't want to miss out on any of the gold, any of the kisses from Heaven that's being worked out of the roughness in my human experience. I was pretty reserved with my love before Gian went Home, not intentionally, but maybe just quietly. I didn't know what I know now. I've been cracked wide open since then. Sometimes, it seems the gold is buried super deep, and some days, I wonder if I'm looking in the wrong area altogether. Then, as soon as I pause for a breath and look up, there it is —a glimmery promise showing up as an answered prayer, love, and laughter in both of our daughters' lives, a memory of Gian shared by a friend, kindness of a stranger, a gift given at the perfect moment, the peace that sweeps in unexpectedly, a baby's laughter, a heart-shaped something or other on the ground or in the sky—a rainbow. Every moment holds promise...curiously enough, even the lead Prosecutor (Kelly) of the case shared that Gian continues to impact her life and the lives of her loved ones in practical ways. She is acutely aware that she is watching her own eighteen-year-old son thriving and enjoying football in the same way that Gian did. She's gone as far as confronting a dear friend's unsafe drinking and driving by sharing the details of Ms. M.'s driving history and the crash. Kelly chose to share pictures of Gian with her friend, and this dear friend allowed Gian's life to impact her beautifully. She's chosen to call an Uber™ since hearing his story. Really, she chose to be impacted by Kelly's story. Gian is part of Kelly's story now, too. I pray that Gian has changed this dear friend's trajectory forever and ever. He certainly has changed mine.

Choosing to be tender toward life and to be impacted by each other is brave, worthy work. Not because we feel brave but **because we do it while we're afraid**.

As a result of the crash, and in the years since I have prayed for justice and about justice, it's become clear that justice happens between us, not necessarily due to a Judge's evaluation of the evidence and interpretation of the laws. Justice, rightness, **and the holding of a stranger's life as precious is a heart stance**. So, for a while now, I've been praying for all the hearts in all the homes. Whether the home is under a bush or is a penthouse, I've been praying that every heart in every home is calibrated to Heaven. Among other things, humanity would develop a holy fear of mistreating, misleading, and trampling one of God's beloveds. We are all His beloveds.

Martin Luther King, Jr. shared, "Injustice anywhere is a threat to justice everywhere. We are caught in an inescapable network of mutuality, tied in a single garment of destiny. Whatever affects one directly affects all indirectly."[vii]

Finding the Gold

What are the natural transactions on Earth that you are wondering about? Are you looking heavenward for the answer or the impact? How are you being changed by what you cannot undo? How are you becoming love for the world around you, creating space for Heaven, and engaging justice for your loved ones?

SEVEN

So Much Joy!

MY LAUGHTER HAD BEEN CHANGED BY THE ONE WHO SITS IN THE HEAVENS AND LAUGHS.

Joy is the serious business of heaven.
~ C. S. Lewis

Zero facades happening here. It's not all heavy lifting. Joy became evident in my life, even as happiness disappeared for a time.

"I created you to know joy unspeakable. . . . Joy is much deeper than what happiness brings. Joy defies trials. It dares to laugh, even when hell is closing in," wrote Brian Simmons and Gretchen Rodriguez in *I hear His Whisper, Encounter God's Heart for You*.

The authors discuss the extreme and distinct difference between happiness and joy. In the absence of all things that create a happy existence, the joy of the Lord is a gift born out of His love for us and, as a result, of His awareness that we would NEED His encouragement. He knew we would need Heavenly inspired help to deal with the storms of life, the attacks we would face against our very identities, our faith, our hope, our futures, and our **happiness**. Not only is God ever present with us, but He is only radically good, and it is safe to anticipate goodness from Him.

As parents, we've experienced so much joy, shared a ton of laughter, and felt deep satisfaction throughout our children's lives. We still do! There's no effort required to tap into that goodness, especially the hard-fought goodness that follows challenges, and to stir up gratitude. While the sorrows of parenthood are also present, they are no more significant than the beauty of all that has gone VERY well, of all that has been and is good, and dare I say, *golden*.

We have chosen to allow all that has gone *well* to remain affixed to joy. My joy is much like a plumb line leading straight to Heaven that runs through every nook and cranny of my heart...and I have a hopeful expectation for goodness continuing in the lives of our children as Heaven invades all of our lives and the Glory that awaits us for eternity. God promises to work all things out for our good and His Glory. The good will have to be VERY good.

Yielded pain can be healed, although wholeness doesn't always look like returning to the previous standard or normal.

My old joy felt like it left or died with Gian, along with my every ounce of happiness. It happens. Shortly thereafter, a rugged beast and true-north force began to well up in my heart. I had no idea this sort of joy existed. This joy has no requirement of happy situations, positive coincidences, stars lining up perfectly, or my recipes turning out well. This was a deep-dwelling, fierce force. It was not that my old joy was counterfeit or flimsy; it just didn't survive my new life.

Sometimes, my joy feels inappropriate, as it frequently drives me to laughter and unwarranted peace when things go wrong. This new joy provoked my hope in strange ways and has made a few friends uncomfortable, as rolls of laughter have been my response to relatively small inconveniences like flat tires. The little and big pains of life are still targets for goodness, in my estimation. My laughter had been changed by the One who sits in the heavens and laughs. He laughs at His enemies, and our enemies are His, too. Laughter and interrupting joy can be super strange to witness, especially when there's no logical circumstance. It is also strange when I consider this mystery in light of Gian's short life. Had my old joy not gone, I would not have identified this new fiery *thing* as joy at all. Joy does have a life of its own, and allowing it to continue to influence us has buffered our hearts and minds in curious ways. I believe we've had a choice in that, but we are not responsible for it. Our joy didn't originate with us. We honor joy as it shows up in both the big and in the slight and glimmery ways, like the sunrise each morning. Acknowledging joy when we feel or see it even off in the distance as a hint of its presence has become a regular practice. What we focus on increases. We let joy do what joy does and embrace it. Our joy is honest.

A very wise and kind counselor recommended that when I recognize joy, I should pause, pay attention to the time, and just enjoy it for as long as it lasts. Not that joy has to lift, but if it does lift, notice the time again and note how long joy was present, then tuck the experience in my heart for future visits. When revisiting with joy and the memory of its impact, then try to expand the sense of joy in regard to time. For instance, I recognized joy that lasted in an upfront type of way for about twenty minutes. When I decided to visit the joy that I had tucked in my heart for another time, I practiced remembering the sensation of joy while being aware of the time; I stayed in those moments again and added two more minutes, kind of like working joy muscles.

It is both/and.

I used to believe that we could experience just one emotion, one feeling at a time, and that only a positive emotion would be *right* or divinely inspired. I believed wrong! We are proof that pure joy, deep sorrow, seething anger, unquenchable love, and devotion (feel free to add to the list) can and do coexist. Much like fruit salad. Chunks of this, slices of that, all mixed together, with the juices running together. The different flavors and textures don't contradict each other; **they provide fullness** and, maybe, even context. Otherwise, you'd just have fruit.

As Grama Gina said, "They bring their love with them." They also spur joy in uniquely individualized ways.

Genna Belle and Gian are 21 months apart. Dadio, Gian, and I celebrated Belle's birth and welcomed her completely. Suddenly becoming big brother, our young prince made it perfectly clear that she was his baby!...AND as enthralled as I was with our beautiful baby girl, I was so sad that my tiny son (complete with stinky binky and blonde curls) was no longer *the* baby. Gian was still so little. The same RN that delivered Belle assured me that it would be OK, "they'll never know a time without each other." True, and not in the way we imagined...I remember laying infant Belle on the living room floor one morning. I walked away for just a second and returned to find Gian holding her up into the air by her ankles! He innocently smiled behind his stinky binky as she peacefully and rather happily dangled in her brother's unusually strong grip! I shouldn't have been surprised, really. Jeff and I had given him a "baby" to practice with before Belle was born, and he was adamant that he could carry his "baby" by her feet! Our Zosia followed Belle twenty-six months later and completed our little family with her chubby "ninja baby" antics! Dadio and I were perfectly outnumbered as our three peas quickly became friends and accomplices in some wildly silly, good moments full of belly laughing and innocent joy.

Interestingly, Gian would continue to carry or throw me or his sisters over his shoulders when he thought this was the best way to be helpful. He and one of his sisters were caught in a downpour, so he picked her up and threw her over his shoulders to RUN home! One day, he and I were visiting friends at a park, and on our way to the car after our goodbyes, I mentioned being ready to be off my feet, so he scooped me up into his arms and carried me princess-style down the block. His grip on me tightened as I tried to squirm out of his hold. He said, "It's OK, momma, let me carry you." I'm so grateful I let him carry me then. Memories are treasures to us. They carry us, really.

No doubt, 2015 will always be a significant year for us. When I look back at that final year together, I am drawn to memories of shared laughing, massive lunch-making episodes, wrestling matches on the living room floor, early morning scrambles piling into Gian's truck for the drive to school, storytelling, group hugs, and kisses. I remember peaking from the kitchen to catch our three gems in a tickle fight, laughing at each other's goofiness, or even the sweetness of just quietly sitting close. In my imagination, I can almost hear them together. Those three had only known life together as peas in a pod and tried (more successfully in some moments than others) to enjoy each other's presence. In my own estimation, I am the richest of Mommas, having such a joy-infused life, much like the art of Kintsugi.

In early 2016, I was introduced to the Japanese art of *precious scars*, called Kintsugi. Rather than throw out broken pottery, the artist binds the broken pieces back together as a way of honoring the pottery's journey even to near destruction. Gold, silver, and other metals are used in the repair process. Although the piece has been broken, it is still seen as useful, and the breaks have become part of the value and part of history. For me, this is what it looks like to draw the goodness of God to all my brokenness until what was not functional is shining golden. The breaks became part of the beauty. I've committed to the lifelong process of becoming completely redeemed, golden, and full of glimmering joy...the breaks become precious scars that serve to reveal God's love, healing, and goodness through them. Not all scars are healed in the same way. These types of scars, the ones that have been impacted by the goodness and golden Glory of God, are NOT for hiding. These scars are valuable to Him and tell a story that will help others come into healing and wholeness, too. This is one way joy for mourning[i] is made tangible, valuable, and appreciable. Because we have mourned, He is giving us His joy.

JOY CONTINUES AS MY PLUMB LINE, MY GUIDE, AND I want it to shine golden in all the places that could not possibly be held together without Heaven's presence.

My prayer sometimes sounds like this:

Let our lives be so GOLDEN...let the broken places be filled with the goodness of Heaven, with unreasonable joy, with all that is true, pure, lovely, and miraculous. Let the joy that Gian lives in, the joy that propelled Jesus, that joy that has sustained us, increase in us and cause it to flow through us. Cause the joy to shine through the fragmented areas to reveal Heaven. To reveal the goodness of God. Let the recipe of Glory and redemption nourish and beautify every chipped corner and sheared edge. May truth, innocence, and hope bind together the areas that have been utterly destroyed by our own choices and those of others. Let the honesty of our lives and the lives of our children draw curious onlookers to apprehend for themselves the promises of a good God. May our devastation work for overwhelmingly GOOD goodness in our lives and in the lives of everyone we come in contact with. Finally, let redemption and joy have their perfect work in us so that Jesus would have His full reward.

More complicated breaks hold the potential to reveal more Glory, more joy, more gold in us, and FOR us to work through us.

Gold serves as a witness to the beauty that remains. It is the reality of Heaven's redemptive, restorative, and healing nature that brings the broken places to wholeness while honoring the break. Nothing is wasted. Not everything that is healed is erased. Some scars do completely fade away, while others don't. We can't force either result. Consider how Jesus kept the holes in His hands and His pierced side when He returned to His disciples after the resurrection. This is how some of them recognized Him, yet it wasn't Jesus' injuries that defined Him, the moment, or the enormity of His accomplishments. Quite the opposite.

Years following the crash, a dear friend of G's chose to enter the Police force. K has shared with us that his desire to pursue this career comes directly from his love for Gian and his desire to make a difference in the local community. K is doing just that.

During a routine traffic stop, K asked to see the driver's license and registration. When this individual was unable to produce his documentation, he gave a name for K to enter into the computer system. K did the search for the name given by the driver, and Gian's name came up! K followed what he felt was Gian's guidance, which yielded the incident at the high school describing the drug exchange he reported. Along with the record of the drug deal, photos of the students involved were included. K was able to determine that the driver was not the person he reported himself to be. The driver eventually provided his real name, which led to an arrest.

This same K gifted me with an honorary dance at his own wedding. Sharing that dance with him and his beautiful, gracious momma was something I'll never ever forget. He just smiled as I cried and kissed his face.

Truly, nothing is wasted. Not one of the hard, devastating, infuriating, confusing, painful moments, days, or years is wasted.

Jesus is our redemption, and He alone makes restoration possible. Just as the gold answers and fills the broken places in the Kintsugi practice, the work of the cross perfectly addressed our need for a Savior, our need for wholeness. Jesus bought our liberation, our deliverance, our healing. Redemption makes all things new and is the means for the restoration of all that was stolen from us. The process of redemption and restoration is on Heaven's timeline, and the impact of Heaven on our brokenness will have lifelong implications. I am certain there's no other Healer, no other way to wholeness this side of Heaven.

Western culture would have us hurry up and be OK while simultaneously encouraging us to stay trapped in trauma and/or victimization by placing tags of identity on us, tying us to the wounds of our past and present. Neither option is healthy, or leads to the kind of justice, wholeness, GOLD, freedom, or goodness our souls were designed for and crave. Our souls need to be attended to. We can have beauty for our ashes, but this requires an exchanging of sorts, not a holding onto, and an inviting of the Creator of the universe into the broken areas. It's my job to invite Him into my ash heaps and give Him permission to do what only He can. The bigger the ash heap, the greater the beauty.

Choosing to allow joy to be present was and is intentional and sometimes exhausting, especially while grief and the heaviness of our loss were so new, raw, and jarring. However, my little family and I chose to not chase joy away but to recognize its presence and acknowledge the relief it brought as laughter, peace, or silliness interrupted our pain-filled moments. Joy happened in us, around us, and through us, quite honestly, very organically. And we lost a few friends in the process of our transparency, which is OK. Attempting to force joy is like forcing gas (a fart). It could be a mistake. Don't do it!

For me, joy is often right there with the fullness of what is happening in my heart, whatever that is.

Within a few months, acquaintances and coworkers began to make comments like, "Gian would want you to be happy." My reply was typically, "Oh, Gian does make me happy! He also values my honesty." I love that Gian wants the best for me, AND I was suffering especially early on. Pushing away suffering because it is unwanted does not eliminate the source of the pain. The undertone of this message sounded to me like, "I am intimidated and uncomfortable with the intensity of your suffering, and I want it to stop. Make your suffering stop so I can be comfortable imagining your life." It is worth noting that I wasn't *typically* sobbing uncontrollably in public. That only happened on rare occasions. I brushed my hair, did my makeup, put on clean and appropriate clothing for work, and I struggled. Fake smiling is, well, fake.

No one and nothing is bettered by pretending. On many mornings, I practice how to honestly answer the ever-anticipated and well-intended greeting, "How are you?" To respond with, "I'm good." Or "great!" feels like a nauseating, bold-faced lie and an utter violation of my heart. I know, it sounds extreme. Because it is!

What feels true to me most mornings is "grateful." So I prepared myself to answer the "How are you today?" question with "Grateful. I am grateful." Positivity's emphasis is warranted and only when practiced authentically.

A Note on Toxic Positivity:

> *"How to Avoid Toxic Positivity" by Jay Vallotton (Instagram Aug 15, 2022)*
>
> *..." Toxic positivity takes positive thinking to an over generalized extreme. This attitude doesn't just stress the importance of optimism; it minimizes and denies any trace of human emotions that aren't strictly happy or positive.*
>
> *Toxic positivity can actually harm people who are going through difficult times. Rather than being able to share genuine human emotions and gain unconditional support, people find their feelings dismissed, ignored, or outright invalidated...show support to yourself and others by being AUTHENTIC."*
>
> — HOW TO AVOID TOXIC POSITIVITY" BY JAY VALLOTON, INSTAGRAM AUG 15TH, 2022

Jay provided the following examples* as loving and easy swaps to help us really express what we often mean to say but are lacking the right words. His language is so kind and grace-filled. God knows I've learned the hard way to be so much more intentional with my own words.

*See the Positivity Table for toxic positivity and healthy, non-toxic alternatives to say to people walking through trauma.

TOXIC POSITIVITY	NON-TOXIC ALTERNATIVES
JUST STAY POSITIVE!	**I'm listening.**
GOOD VIBES ONLY!	**I'm here no matter what.**
IT COULD BE WORSE.	**That must be really hard.**
EVERYTHING HAPPENS FOR A REASON.	**Sometimes bad things happen.**
FAILURE ISN'T AN OPTION.	**How can I help?**
HAPPINESS IS A CHOICE.	**Failure is part of life.**
BE STRONG!	**Your feelings are valid.**

I have found the grounding effect of joy and authenticity can be practiced in gratitude. Gratitude expands our focus to include all that is well and gives voice to whom and what we are grateful for. To be clear, I am not grateful for many things in this life, and I refuse to be dishonest about any of that ever. However, I am grateful that 1 Thessalonians 5:18 says, "In all things give thanks." This verse is **NOT** saying we are to be grateful *for* all things and give thanks. Massive difference. In the midst of going through hell in a handbag, I was able to thank God for sustaining me, for loving me, for keeping me from evolving into a raging alcoholic, and for protecting the world from my fury. Thank You, God, for that.

However, practicing gratitude has allowed me to focus my thinking and heart in rather life-saving ways. That's not an exaggeration. Without gratitude, I could easily slide into the pit of despair, become thoroughly consumed by all that is wrong, and lose all hope. It's still true that my joy is an unruly and often distracting beast, but it doesn't just bob around aimlessly. Can a person be joy-filled and hopeless or hopeful and joyless? I don't think so, but there is an ebb and flow. Joy and Hope are a pair, kind of like conjoined twins. Gratitude is one of the glues that hold them together. Independent but connected. Joy and practicing gratitude will stir hope.

Joy isn't delicate. Hope isn't aimless.

Gratitude, though, will breathe life into joy and hope and stir both.

This can be as simple as recognizing a flower beginning to bloom even with frost on the ground. There's no denying it's cold outside, yet the flower is EVIDENCE that new life *is happening*. It's good to massage our hope, our joy, and our gratitude. What we focus on increases...and laughing is such good, pure, cheap medicine.

Practicing gratitude for me looks like this:

"I am grateful for the cool breeze that's breaking up the heat right now."

"I am grateful our girls have found love and are thriving."

"I am grateful for Jeff's kindness."

"I am grateful that while I miss Gian, no one can ever hurt him again. I am grateful he is completely safe."

"I am grateful that ice cubes are cold."

"I am grateful that today, I am one day closer to Gian."

"I am grateful for a photo of the lighted G sign from niece Kayleigh taken at a museum in London called "God's Junkyard,"

"I am grateful that my lungs still breathe in and out, that each borrowed breath is returning to the Creator of it all."

Most days, I am fully camped out like a determined squatter on all that I am grateful for, and sure enough, joy is right there in the midst of everything. Focusing long on what is well doesn't mean I am shutting my eyes, plugging my ears, and ignoring the world around me or the things that hurt, far from it. With eyes, ears, and heart wide open, I am leaning hard into Heaven with gratitude and joyfully anticipating that the things I am not grateful for will be overwhelmed by the goodness of God. I am anticipating and expecting to see the goodness of God in the land of the living.[ii]

The author of Hebrews 12:2 says, "For the joy set before Him, He endured . . . ." [iii] Jesus chose to lean into what was ahead of Him, to endure all that He did for us. I chose to lean in, too. And **I still choose to lean into** His joy that is now full. Relying on His joy, His presence, His love for Gian, and His love for me continues to be the only way forward for me.

Finding the Gold

Since joy is the serious business of Heaven, how are you welcoming joy? How are you working your joy muscles? What would you look like if the gold substance of Heaven filled all of your broken places? What are you focusing on? Is your focus helping to stir your hope? What simple thing can you do to increase your gratitude?

EIGHT

Addressing The Court

IGNORANCE DOESN'T PROTECT; NOR DOES FEAR.

Never forget that justice is
what love looks like in public.
~ Cornel West

Driving is not a right—it's a responsibility; it's a privilege.

Sometimes, the reality (or discovered evidence) is flat-out ugly, and ignorance is not bliss. Ignorance doesn't protect us. Neither does fear.

There were laws broken on the night of the collision, and ultimately, the responsible driver plead guilty to the charge of vehicular homicide. The following is the statement I was permitted to read aloud to the Judge for her sentencing. This statement was actually read during the second court appearance that we were invited to attend and participate in. No one else from the Prosecution side was allowed to speak during this final sentencing. (I've chosen not to share my statement prepared for the first court appearance in October 2016 because that statement is too messy and says too much for the purposes of this book.)

My peace was under serious attack. All I could do was say, "Help, Jesus, I cannot face the Court without Your help and without Your version of peace. You're the only one who can make *this* good. It's going to have to be astronomically good to be considered good at all."

Instantly, this verse came to mind, "Be anxious for nothing; but in everything by prayer and supplication with thanksgiving let your request be made known to God. And the peace of God, which surpasses all understanding, will guard your hearts and minds through Christ Jesus." Philippians 4:6-7.

Even now, I am encouraged to hold everything loosely and to stay in conversation...to keep thanking Him for His love for us, His care for what we care about, His version of justice, and to talk to Him about what it looks like for Heaven to invade this moment. As I listen, pause, and lean in, peace washes over me. And there have been moments when His peace simply enabled me to not nervously vibrate off of a chair.

As I sat on the bench in the courtroom that day, looking at my hands while my guts shimmied...I heard my Lord say, "The roar of a lion will be released in your whisper." He knows just what to say. I wanted to be bold, strong, and confident, and even though I dressed well and put makeup on, I felt like I could barely get my words out through my tears and shaking. Our desire for some version of justice for Gian, for the others in the crash, for us hadn't lessened.

ADDRESSING THE COURT

"Thank you for the opportunity to address the court this morning, Your Honor.

I feel it appropriate to begin by clearing the air.

I have chosen to not attend hearings after Ms. M. entered the Electronic Home Monitoring program for several reasons. I've wanted her to

STAND ON HER OWN BEHALF, UNINFLUENCED BY OUR PRESENCE, TO SEE WHAT SHE WOULD DO. TO GET A SENSE OF HOW INTENTIONAL SHE WOULD CHOOSE TO BE WITH FOLLOWING THE CONTRACT WHEN NO-ONE IS LOOKING, HOW DEEPLY SHE WANTS TO CHANGE AND REMAIN PRESENT FOR HER CHILDREN, AND TO SEE JUST HOW SERIOUSLY SHE WOULD TAKE THIS OPPORTUNITY. INTERNAL CHANGE IS EVIDENCED BY OUR BEHAVIOR, BY OUR CHOICES, AND CHANGE IS OBSERVABLE.

OUR FAMILY HAS INTENTIONALLY MAINTAINED SPACE BETWEEN US AND MS. M. I QUITE HONESTLY DON'T WANT TO SEE HER. NOT HERE AND NOT IN PUBLIC. I HAVE TO SHIELD MY HEART. MY DAILY, MINUTE-TO-MINUTE EXPERIENCE IS BRUTALLY PAINFUL. BEING HERE ISN'T THERAPEUTIC FOR ME. SYMPATHY, PATRONIZING, AND WEAK APOLOGIES MAKE MY STOMACH TURN. I FEEL SUCH A LACK OF EVIDENCE THAT MS. M. IS IMPACTED AT ALL BY HAVING ENDED GIAN'S LIFE.

EACH HEARING WE HAVE ATTENDED, AND THEN WITH EVERY UPDATE OR NOTIFICATION OF UPCOMING HEARINGS, WE HAVE CONTINUED TO EXPERIENCE DAYS OF HEIGHTENED ANXIETY, NAUSEA, VOMITING, ANGER, PHYSICAL PAIN, DEPRESSION, FLASHBACKS, NIGHTMARES, SUDDEN FLOODS OF HARD EMOTIONS, AND INCESSANT TEARS FOR DAYS PRIOR, THE DAY OF, AND FOR THE DAYS FOLLOWING. JEFF, THE GIRLS, AND I HAVE MISSED 100'S OF SCHOOL AND UNREIMBURSED WORK HOURS, AS A DIRECT RESULT OF THE LEGAL PROCEEDINGS ALONE. WE ARE EASILY TRIGGERED, DERAILED, AND, AT TIMES, ALARMINGLY INCAPACITATED. GIAN BELONGS TO US JUST AS HE ALWAYS HAS! THIS IS INCREDIBLY PAINFUL FOR US –

THE ADAGE, "TIME HEALS ALL WOUNDS," IS A LIE.

Time doesn't heal anything – it does serve as a kind of marinade, however, and we have, in essence, been plunged into a 2yr and 10mos reality, a marinade Ms. M. created for us. In response to the Defense's assumption that we must have moved on...Your Honor, there is nowhere for us to go. Move on to what??

I am, and will always be, the mother of three children. Three. For the rest of my life, I am the mother of three children. For the rest of my life, I will wake up to manage the impact that Ms. M.'s negligent choices have had on my life, on my family, and on our loved ones. For the rest of our lives, we will marinate in the reality that Ms. M. created for us.

Please forgive my oversimplification...but when my kids were little, we practiced "time-outs." They knew how much time was set on the timer and they understood what behavior changes were necessary to come back to the group, to come back to the fun, as we used to say. Occasionally, one of them needed more time to work on an attitude or behavior that got them in time out in the first place. We would reset the timer with a phrase like, "Your choices are letting me know you're not quite ready to join the fun." "We'll miss you and look forward to being with you when you can manage yourself well."

I feel like the timer needs to be reset, Your Honor. The 5yr Electronic Home Monitoring program is incredibly brief in comparison to the lifetime of influence Ms. M. has had and will have on us. Maybe the enormity escapes her.

Perhaps she hasn't been impacted enough to be ready to change.

The contract allowed for heightened awareness, care, and acceptance of responsibility, diligence, and intentional behavior, leaving absolutely no room for doubt or added sorrow in being able to prove deep commitment. Violating the contract sends a powerful message. One of Gian's sisters describes it as "a slap in the face."

It seems nearly 3yrs of valuable time with her children has not helped her take ownership of her behavior. The message to me is that she doesn't take any of this seriously, that she is trying to see what kind of wiggle room she can establish and how she can bend the requirements. As if she is asking, "Is this REALLY what it says?" or "Let's see how far I can push it..."

For these reasons, please restart the timer.

Please provide the time for her to connect with ownership of her choices. She may not be using alcohol, but that was not entirely the point of the electronic home monitoring. The point of the monitoring is also to provide an opportunity for the rehabilitation to occur that's needed for her to rejoin society safely, all the while caring for her own children. To keep her off the roads for as long as possible. She's been provided an extravagant, gracious option in response to robbing my son of his life and to avoid trial. We would have loved to have had those days with Gian!

In my opinion, Washington State, unfortunately, miscalculated when granting Ms. M.

leniency in response to her negligence, even before she was of legal driving age. If she had been allowed to experience the consequences of her choices all those years ago, at the very beginning, with the very first infraction, perhaps she would have been convinced of her ability to powerfully influence her own future, her children's quality of life, and the world around her.

None of us would be here today but for her driving privileges. My beautiful son would be here, free to live his life, our family would be complete. We would not be here today. My son might still be alive if Ms. M. had made a different choice and had established different patterns of behavior. Past failures, whatever they may be, cannot be undone. But this opportunity now, Your Honor, if you allow her to have it, could help her experience the consequences of her negligent choices. And to process it all with the gift of time. Allow her to marinate.

Ms. M. killed my son by driving nearly 3x's the posted speed limit, the exact same speed she had been ticketed for several times in prior years. The EXACT speed. She picked up her newborn, drove about 5 blocks, swerved to avoid another car in her path, and demolished a car stopped at her red light. Our Gian was in that car.

She claims to have been sober and sleepy, which is more alarming than if she were intoxicated!

I believe our laws have allowed her to continue in this manner and not experience the consequences necessary for true change to occur until her driving pattern resulted in my son's death. True change has evidence. Adhering to her own agreement would be just the very first bit of evidence that would indicate a change has occurred or is occurring. Following directions shows compliance and an understanding of the magnitude of the irreparable damage she has done to our family.

If it were miraculously possible, I'd wholeheartedly accept Gian back in trade for Ms. M. receiving the lightest possible sentence. Truly, I only want my son.

My needs are very basic. I need my family, and I am consumed by a furious, fiery love for them. I am just as committed, just as focused, just as infuriated, sickened, only now I am somehow more carefree, stronger, and clear about it all. Since November 6th, 2015, I am 100 times more intentional and transparent. I no longer am concerned by the opinion of anyone other than my God, and I live with the constant tension of being pulled between Heaven and earth. I am so keenly aware that today is all that I have to offer, so I offer it well. I no longer mince words, and I don't waste anything anymore. I am not afraid of people, or death, or suffering... and my burning desire continues to be to manage myself in a way that I can influence my children to live beautifully strong lives, by having access to their hearts. That my Darlings will be encouraged to show up stronger every day. To show up honest, forgiving, innocent, generous, and with boldness to stand upright and to take their rightful places as children of

Light. To be governed by unrelenting love. And they are.

I am earning the right to be my children's friend.

And I want who was removed from my life, without my consent. I want Gian to be returned to my present experience on this earth. I want to help Gian paint his living room walls. I want to celebrate as he asks the love of his life to be his wife; I want to dance with him at his wedding; I want to help raise his babies; I want his babies to grow up with his sisters' babies; I want to watch him and his big beautiful brood of cousins laugh and be silly together again, I want to cheer Gian on as a husband, a father, an uncle...I want to continue our deepening friendship. I want to listen to his heartbeat through his rough denim shirt. I want to hear his voice in my ear again. I want my family to be whole again. I want my three children to be together in the same room again. I want to entirely enjoy holidays, Gian's birthday, every family gathering, every celebration, the entire fall season, every 6th, 7th, and 8th of every month, I want my husband's son back; I want my daughters' big brother back. If she could just do that. Just give him back.

Since she cannot return to me who she has taken from me, please allow her to pay the highest price possible. The very highest price possible, by providing her the very most time in prison possible.

Regarding closure, no.

Time in prison is an answer to Ms. M.'s behavior, to her responsibility in Gian's death. Maybe

> PRISON TIME WILL PROVIDE HER CLOSURE. CERTAINLY NOT OURS. WE WILL ONLY BE SATISFIED WHEN WE ARE WITH GIAN AGAIN."

After taking my seat again, Ms. M. asked permission to respond to me. She chose to say, "I know you hate me." Interesting choice of words, and incidentally not at all accurate. I have and continue to forgive her, whether she ever apologizes or not. My forgiveness is mine to steward and is independent of her asking for it or attempting to earn it. This side of heaven, I may never have the gift of her sincere acknowledgement of her choices and responsibility for our loss.

There is a lot that I am choosing to not share about the legal details and the responsible driver. You'll just have to trust me when I say that the facts (discovered evidence) are ugly. Part of the back story of this statement is months and months of violations and special requests for exceptions to the home monitoring contract she chose and signed. She had been back to court for these violations and exemption requests, and because we were encouraged not to feel pressure to attend these dates, we didn't. However, in our absence, the Defense accused us of having moved on and no longer caring about the case, insinuating that the importance of the case no longer existed because we hadn't attended. I am grateful for Kelly Montgomery (K. Mont, as her friends call her), the Prosecuting Attorney's extreme dedication to the case, to the laws, and her compassionate commitment to us for Gian. We trusted her guidance and recommendations completely, and when the Defense took cheap shots at us, she continued to be professionally responsive while putting the Defense in his place. She is a mother, too, after all.

Kelly later shared with me that she felt the real wreckage was in discretion. In other words, that our choices and discretion are the wreckage. Thought-provoking, isn't it? Our choices and thinking create realities for us, but not only us. It's actually more likely that we end up hurting other people with our choices. She went on to explain that people get lost in the fog, and part of her job is to blow the fog away for everyone to be able to see clearly. She knows well that people--that we--are fallible.

The truth really does set us free. It is not a kindness, or merciful to allow the world around us to continue in that fog. Even if life in the fog is comfortable, familiar, and numbing. The truth is life in that fog is harming us and putting us in danger. Sometimes, mercy enters our lives as a wake-up call or as a second chance. Truth and mercy can be painful in these moments. They are intended to get our attention, to get us to pause and do something different. Living with each other in mind has its risks. I risk my own wants not being satisfied for the well-being of the one in front of me, next to me, and entering following me.

G's Dadio knows this reality personally and professionally. For the last twenty-seven years, he has been in the child and family social work community trenches, fighting for our children.

The following is called "A Return to Civility," which expresses the heart of Jeff, an engaged, loving, fierce father who has fought, fought, and fought for other people's children and his own.

"A Return to Civility"

JEFF KING

WHY THE GOLDEN RULE BECAME GOLDEN.

"Many civilizations throughout history have had their own versions of the Golden Rule, the law of reciprocity in some religions. Treating others as you would want to be treated seems to have been a common theme throughout history. Psychologically, it involves a person empathizing with others. Philosophically, it involves a person perceiving their neighbor also as *I* or *self*. Sociologically, "love your neighbor as yourself "[i] is applicable between individuals, between groups, and also between individuals and groups.

If you are anything like me, you can probably make a very good list of how you **do *not* want** to be treated, but the list of ***how*** you do want to be treated may be a bit fuzzier. I don't expect everyone to love me, much less like me, but it would be nice if there were some way for people with vastly different backgrounds, therefore vastly different perspectives, and beliefs to get along.

Oh Yes, CIVILITY. Civility is defined as formal politeness and courtesy in behavior or speech. Latin *civilitas*, from civilis' relating to citizens' (see civil).[ii] In early use, the term denoted the state of being a citizen and hence good citizenship or orderly behavior. The sense of *politeness* arose in the mid-16th century.[iii]

When people transitioned from Hunter/ Gatherers to farming and communal living, certain rules and codes of conduct needed to be developed for the well-being of the individual and the good of the whole community. These communities developed over many years. We look back and refer to them as Civilizations.

The Civil Code of Conduct from Roman times[iv] would certainly seem out of place today. But maybe there are things we can learn from Ancient Civilizations to help us define what it means to be civil in today's age.

Before George Washington became the first president of the United States of America, he, as a young boy, wrote a publication called *The Rules of Civility and Decent Behaviour In Company and Conversation.*[v] Washington's book covered 110 rules on civility with a primary message to instill good manners. Seems like this topic has been around for a while.

So, how can we define our Golden Rule,[vi] today? How can we demonstrate civility to one another and rescue our society from the precipice of decay?

Remembering that our thoughts can only be demonstrated through our words and actions, what simple actions, repeated by millions of like-minded people, would demonstrate to the world that our society can and will Return to CIVILITY?

Remembering that it is okay to disagree with someone without demonizing them is a good start. Remember that the person driving in front of you has many things going on in their lives as well and that your presumed emergencies are no more important than theirs. Remembering that kindness goes so very far in developing a sense of goodwill and community.

Civility goes beyond mere toleration of each other but implies respect for **humankind**, which requires a certain degree of harmony and opposes violence in order to remain civil.

Recently, Dadio rediscovered a birthday card he gave to Gian on his fifteenth birthday. His message to his son reads,

> GIAN,
>
> THE LOVE A FATHER HAS FOR HIS FIRSTBORN SON IS SOMETHING PEOPLE HAVE TRIED TO DESCRIBE THROUGHOUT HISTORY.
>
> UNFORTUNATELY, ADEQUATE WORDS HAVE NEVER BEEN CREATED TO FULLY EXPRESS THE LOVE, PRIDE, CONCERN, AND FAITH THAT LIVE INSIDE A FATHER'S HEART.
>
> I WISH FOR YOU EVERY EXCELLENT THING YOUR HEART DESIRES. AS A FATHER, I CANNOT GIVE YOU ALL OF THESE THINGS, BUT I HOPE TO PASS ON TO YOU THE WILL AND TENACITY TO ENTER FORTH INTO THE WORLD AND CLAIM THOSE THINGS AS YOUR OWN.
>
> I LOVE YOU, AND GOD BLESS YOU IN EVERY WAY!

Dadio's heart hasn't changed toward his boy, our daughters, or the children he continues to support. He works diligently to shift the family dynamic to one of trust, safety, kindness, gentleness, hope, and healthy connection, with an understanding that our second chances eventually run out.

Finding the Gold

How are you practicing being justice for those in your sphere of influence through the lens of love? What does loving your neighbor as yourself look like? How can you love yourself better? What needs/appetites need to be addressed in the world around you (or personally) that conflict with the "Golden Rule?"

NINE

Second Chances Or Mercy Versus Nineth Chance

UNSANCTIFIED MERCY AND LIFE AS FREE WILL AGENTS

Keep your heart with all vigilance,
for from it flow the springs of life.
~ Proverbs 4:23 ESV

Everything we do, every choice we make, everything we say originates in our hearts first. We can literally observe the well-being of an individual's heart (their true self) by their actions and words. When beauty or generosity (really when any good or terrible *thing* comes out of a person), we can be assured that word or act originated in them before it ever came out of them. Same goes for greed, or selfishness, or bravery, or faith, or gentleness, or love, or sacrifice.

I totally believe in mercy and second chances and have needed them both, and as a self-proclaimed imperfect human, I have both freely and hesitantly handed plenty of mercy and second chances out while simultaneously requesting them for myself. A second chance is only that, however. A second chance is not a 9th chance or a free pass to do it again after the 10th time. That is something else. The value behind a second chance is the opportunity for self-examination, to own the mistake, behavior, accident, or poor choice, and to have a thoughtful do-over. A chance to do *it* right the next time, whatever *it* is. A course correction or even recalibration. I love a good recalibration!

A second chance restores the liberty to try again, with a no-repeat expectation. There's personal ownership in second chances, both in taking one and in giving one.

Second chances are a perfect response in the case of an accident. An accident is defined by Merriam-Webster as an "unforeseen and unplanned event or circumstance, versus calculated risk, which is defined as a hazard or chance of failure whose degree of probability has been reckoned or estimated before some undertaking is entered upon."[i] We watch calculated risk happen before our eyes as street bicyclists choose to share the road, and every time we eat sushi purchased from a gas station. There's a real risk.

An accident looks like tripping over a tree root on a trail, and as you fall and flail, you whack your friend in the face with your to-go coffee cup. That's an accident for both you and your friend. If you can foresee it, anticipate it, plan for it, and prevent it, it is not an accident.

Calculated risk had been displayed by Ms. M, the responsible driver, as she had been ticketed for traveling at exactly 83 mph several times before the collision, and then the black box of her vehicle read 83 mph at the time of impact. That was a choice.

Mercy is a big deal and can be partially described as the kindness, protection, tenderness, gentleness, benevolence, favor, goodness, care, and grace of God[ii]that is free to us and new every single morning...[iii] I'm SO RELIEVED and inspired by that. Mercy is something I am over the moon grateful for, personally and selfishly. I revel in God's mercy every day and am awestruck by how mercy is practiced by regular people every minute of every day.

Practically speaking, mercy can look like moving a snail off of the walking trail and securing its immediate future, at least, by placing it in a secluded grassy patch...and mercy looks like giving a cup of cool water to the thirsty guy with the sign in his hand at the street corner.

Mercy began to show up for me in the form of a co-worker named Shawn. This lady had a crunchy exterior initially, yet as trauma began to make starting and completing normal work for me and all related tasks nearly impossible, Shawn would so kindly, gently, and often silently come alongside me to help. Sometimes with a smile, but most often without one, she would just help. Her mercy took all the anxiety out of those moments for me. She and I both knew I wasn't doing well, wasn't coping well, or breathing well for that matter, but her presence and gentleness communicated more to me than I had words for. She wasn't going to let me fail in my suffering, and I have such a debt of love to her for that. Curious, isn't it that my co-worker stepped in to cover a debt she didn't owe? Mercy is like that.

> *Through the LORD's mercies, we are not consumed because His compassions fail not. They are new every morning; great is Your faithfulness.*
>
> —Lamentations 3:22-24 *NKJV*

His mercies really are new every morning. We look like Him when we are merciful.

Life is kind of like running hurdles; at some point, we all get tired or injured and eventually get stuck. It's so much like making it almost all the way over a hurdle only to have the tip of your second foot not quite make it. Sometimes, we just get stuck with no strength or ability to get unstuck by ourselves...my friend, Shawn, somehow knew when I was "stuck," and she would ever so gently just take my toes off the hurdle and lower my foot to the ground so I could continue to run, or just stumble forward as it was. Such MERCY.

Mercy is strategic.

In response to calculated risk, mercy could look like removing privileges to help ensure the safety of the world around us if we aren't willing to be safe for ourselves. When we demonstrate an unwillingness to take the world around us into consideration, mercy could show up as restraint from an outside presence. Mercy could also provide encouragement to solve challenges and think about our options from an empowered perspective.

Unsanctified mercy is not a biblical term but one I stumbled across (interestingly) just before a discussion with a very influential woman in the legal arena. This conversation happened after the responsible driver was sentenced to prison, and this woman let me know that her concern had rested heavily on the defendant and her ability to pay her legal fees, her ability to get to court-ordered meetings, her ability to fulfill the requirements of her sentence, and continue or secure care for her children. Her list of concerns for the defendant was impressively long and had little to do with what she had done. She believed at the time of our conversation that consequences for the guilty party's pleas or charges should be in accordance with the guilty party's ability to pay and with consideration for how the consequences will impact his or her dependents. I value this woman's honesty, although her words and perspective have been and still are challenging for me.

I asked her if she meant that the laws didn't mean the same thing for people with (perceived) fewer or lesser resources or support... or for mothers. Not all mothers are good. This influential woman didn't believe at that time that everyone should be responsible in the same way for their actions and offenses, that accountability is subjective, essentially saying that some of us aren't worth as much as others. If the consequences of our actions really hurt us, maybe the consequences are too much. Yikes. I suggested that all people on either side of the law should be treated as though they are capable of handling earned repercussions. People are powerful and influential, as demonstrated by our free will, and enough so that we need to be able to own the consequences of those choices. This is the literal value behind the free choice. We literally influence our own world and the world around us by what we choose and by what we don't choose.

In many supreme courts in the United States, a person having driven recklessly and killed someone could be facing murder charges even if their actions weren't motivated by a desire to kill another person. That's an appropriate consequence for ending someone's life.

True mercy is not tolerant of flippant choices or harmful patterned behavior...this is what I meant when I introduced the idea of unsanctified mercy... it's that slimy thing that enables some of us (and offenders) to repeat, and repeat, and repeat. At some point, our human version of mercy has to show up as a boundary that says, "I love you. This stops now." Or, in a community, "your choices are telling me you want or need limitations on your privileges and freedoms."

The humanistic version of compassion without boundaries and rules that will be enforced is risky. When someone is permitted, empowered, or enabled to make dangerous and or illegal choices intentionally, knowingly over and over without correction, without allowing them to experientially own, like REALLY OWN, the responsibility of their adult choices, this creates the illusion of personal exemption.

None of us are exempt.

We all get to choose. We will all be held accountable, at some point, for the things we choose, the words we use, and for the things we don't choose or say. We are allowed and empowered to make decisions for ourselves and the world around us, just like my friend Shawn. Her version of mercy enabled me to keep running even though trauma would have me face-plant both literally and figuratively.

I would like to propose that mercy be the path we choose when encountering humans having a human experience on the planet, whether good, bad, or indifferent, and **not** as the excuse used to offer exemption for the consequences of our powerful influence. Instead, let mercy give water to the thirsty, show kindness to the lonely, take the keys of the intoxicated or otherwise impaired, remove the sharp objects from the toddler, AND help each other confront our excuses for behaving in a manner unbecoming of a prince or princess.

There are people that I love that have been told they drive like assholes. These Dear-hearts know our story intimately, and some of them have chosen to adjust their driving as a result. Some of them haven't.

In a perfect world, we own the consequences of our actions and our choices, but our world is in turmoil, and the innocent frequently pay the highest prices. Please travel gently and with awareness both in life and on the roads. As I see it, true mercy interferes with destructive outcomes by providing an opportunity for personal recalibration. Had Ms. M. accepted her own opportunity for a personal shift all those years ago with her first DUI, our lives would have been dramatically different.

Each of our individual trajectories impacts the world around us.

Finding the Gold

Share a personal recalibration of your own. What did it cost you? How are you working to ensure the important shift in you stays current? Does mercy need to confront you, too? How are you showing up as mercy in the way of protecting your loved ones?

TEN

Victim Panel Statement

"I HAVE THREE CHILDREN."

Mercy says hard, true things.
Mercy protects people.
~ Alanna

The following statement was prepared to share Gian's story as part of a victim panel in Washington State and now with Mothers Against Drunk Driving (MADD) in Arizona. Victims and, or survivors of reckless and drug/alcohol-related collisions are given the opportunity to share their stories with an audience of mostly court-ordered attendees.

Every day, mercy shows up fresh for me and for the world around me. In the fine details of my life story and the lives of so many others, we share our stories in hopes of saving someone and keeping another family out of our club.

To me, it is a kind of mercy to suddenly be surrounded by some of the most beautiful people who have endured a similar kind of traumatic loss and injustice.

For none of us lives to himself, and no one dies to himself.

—Romans 14:7 NKJV

WE ARE ALL LUMPED IN THIS STATEMENT. MALE AND FEMALE ALIKE.

Although the *Victim Impact Panel* gatherings are generally palpably overloaded with the shame and the fear many of these precious ones are carrying because of what they've been caught doing, I feel peaceful and alive in being present with them. Some feel shame because, as a few attendees have expressed, they feel they should have known better and should have done better. Some are afraid of what they are held captive to hear and to see. Some are afraid of being judged beyond how they are already judging themselves. Just a few arrive publicly intoxicated and are then escorted out by the Police Officers in attendance. Sober attendance is required. I was completely blown away the first time I witnessed an attendee be walked out because of substance use at a victim impact panel.

All ages are represented, and while a few of them may make early eye contact with the event coordinator and presenters, the weight of guilt is tangible on some as they sit perched on preset chairs. The opening statements include a kind assurance from the coordinator as he or she clarifies the goal of the event and acknowledges that all of us make choices that we wish we could undo.

Following roughly 45 minutes of statistics and science pertaining to blood alcohol levels, how much of what kind of beverage it takes to impair men and women, the factors involved, and other known impairing substances, the panel speakers are invited one at a time to come forward to share how we have been personally impacted. We are invited to create and share a slide show of our loved ones and bring any other items to help paint a picture of our losses.

So far, each time I've shared our story, my hands shake a little bit, and for some reason, I cry at a different part, and the room is pin-drop silent.

VICTIM PANEL STATEMENT

"Hi...my name is Alanna King, and I might cry.

...before I share. I want to say that I have forgiven her.

Like many moms, I am incredibly proud and so totally in love with my 3 kids. Of all the places motherhood has brought me these last 26 years, I never imagined I would be invited to share, out of my own experience, what it is to survive the most brutally painful reality of my life. The reason I am here with you is because our first-born, my first true love, was killed while stopped at a red light.

Gian was 18yrs old at the time of the collision. Having graduated from a high school in Washington State the June before, he was immediately employed by the Dept of Navy at Puget Sound Naval Shipyard in Shop 56. He was trained as a pipefitter and was thriving! He loved learning from the "crunchy old guys," as he referred to them.

G is our only son and our two daughters' trailblazing, rugged, funny, painfully generous, wildly brave, strong, justice loving, rough and tumbly, silly, battle ready, hero of a big brother.

He made it his mission in life to look for the

GOLD IN PEOPLE. WHILE I'D LOVE TO TAKE SOME CREDIT FOR HOW GIAN CHOSE TO LIVE, I CAN'T. HE MADE HIS OWN CHOICES.

G, WE ARE TOLD BY HIS FRIENDS, TEAMMATES, COWORKERS, FAMILY, AND COMMUNITY MEMBERS, WAS "THAT GUY" AS HE HAD A WAY OF CALLING WHEN YOU NEEDED TO KNOW SOMEONE CARED; HE HAD A WAY OF SHOWING UP WHEN YOU HAD HEAVY LIFTING TO DO. LITERALLY. HE LOVED TO BALE HAY, MOVE BOULDERS, DOWN TREES, AND REPAIR FENCES. HE LOVED HARD WORK, AND HE LOVED TO HELP.

...AND HE HAD A WAY OF SEEING PEOPLE WHO DESPERATELY NEEDED A HUG, A SHOULDER, A SMILE, A LAUGH, A FRIEND, A DEFENDER, OR A SANDWICH. I FOUND OUT AFTER THE CRASH THAT 1 OF THE 3 SANDWICHES HE HAD TO HAVE IN HIS BACKPACK ALWAYS FILLED SOMEONE ELSE'S BELLY. ONE OF THOSE PHONE CALLS WAS TO A TEAMMATE THAT GIAN DIDN'T KNOW WAS PREPARING TO COMMIT SUICIDE BUT ABANDONED HIS PLAN BECAUSE OF GIAN'S CARE. HIS TEAMMATE HAD NO IDEA ANYONE CARED UNTIL GIAN CALLED.

...AND HE HAD A WAY OF SHOWING UP WHEN SOMEONE NEEDED TO BE PROTECTED; HE HAD NO PROBLEM BREAKING UP FIGHTS OR DEFENDING A STRANGER, AND HE WAS A FIRST RESPONDER TO SEVERAL COLLISIONS AND ACCIDENTS IN HIS SHORT LIFE. IN FACT, THE ONLY TIME HE GOT SUSPENDED WAS BECAUSE HE STEPPED IN AS ONE OF HIS TEACHERS WAS BEING MISTREATED BY A FELLOW CLASSMATE. APPARENTLY, THE BULLY FELT CONFRONTED AND AFRAID, AND WHILE HE DID STOP MISTREATING THE TEACHER, HE ALSO FELT THREATENED, SO GIAN GOT A FEW EXTRA DAYS AWAY FROM SCHOOL. I DO LOVE THAT HE DID THE RIGHT THING BY HIS TEACHER AT THAT MOMENT.

From a very young age, G talked about doing something big, something really important with his life, and felt like he needed to do that thing NOW. He and I would talk about what it could look like to lend his strength, to care for, to show up well for the world around him in his daily life. Just months before the crash, as I was passing through his bedroom to drop off laundry, he turned and said to me, "I know I'm going to take the grenade for some people." I asked him what he meant, and he "replied, there's no greater love than to lay down your life for one's friends." He wasn't wrong, but I paused and reminded him of all the ways he could give his life without laying it down in the way he was inferring.

I didn't know until after he had gone that he was living that out. I am so grateful for the flood of stories that washed over us, describing the powerfully beautiful ways Gian chose to participate in life.

And he craved fun! He rode motorcycles, had a quad, loved target shooting, and was a natural with a bow and arrow; he also ran track, wrestled, and played football and lacrosse. Lacrosse was his favorite. We joked that I had hindered his lacrosse game as a little kid by not allowing him to chase his friends with sticks! He wanted to be with his buddies battling, getting muddy, adventuring, laughing. He had a really great sense of humor!

He would have made a fantastic husband, father, and uncle. I am always going to want to dance with him at his wedding. I am always going to want to be a grandmother to his babies, and I will always wonder if his children would've had his bright green eyes. I am always going to recognize the empty place with his sisters as they move forward with their own futures.

Friday, November 6th, 2015, at about 8:30pm, while stopped at a red light, Gian, his girlfriend (who was driving) with her little brother in the back seat, was struck from behind, shoved into the intersection, and hit by 3 additional cars. The person responsible for the collision was a 26-year-old mother of 2 young children, traveling 83mph in a 35mph, .6 miles into her drive. I'll refer to her as Ms. M.

Gian's dad and I had to drive through the crash site just an hour later to get to him at the local hospital. It looked like a bomb went off.

There was no drug or alcohol testing performed at the crash site, and the urine sample collected at the hospital was mistakenly thrown out. We were told the scene was too chaotic for blood to be ordered. She says she may have been tired but was sober. Three investigations later, the findings say it is unlikely she was sleeping. Our lawyers informed us that the crash was not considered an accident. We were told to strike the word accident from our vocabulary,

Here's the thing, legally speaking, when someone is responsible for the death of your kid, that person's business becomes your business. It just does. I NEVER wanted to know that she had 2 prior DUIs, injuring her own child in the 1st and then with a car full of friends in the 2nd. I never wanted to know that she had been ticketed several times for traveling exactly 83mph, had her license suspended for reckless driving, and for driving without insurance. As the details of that night were discovered, it became clear that she had taken the same calculated risk she had chosen several times before.

I don't believe she intended to kill my son, but her intentions didn't prevent Gian or our family from paying the consequences of her choices or the ongoing impact on our daily experience.

Eventually, Ms. M. plead guilty to vehicular homicide to avoid going to trial and served a 32 month sentence, after violating the alternative to sentencing which was a 5yr house arrest contract. She was released from prison just days after Gian's 23rd birthday. I hope prison provided time for some kind of transformation in her, as it did nothing restorative for us. The Supreme Courts of America have limitations and are not capable of issuing true justice. True justice would look like Gian being restored to life on the planet. I will only have justice when he and I are together again. So, I have learned that justice happens between us. Between you and me as we protect each other.

Anyway... Gian's extrication and intubation was ordered by his best friend's grandfather that night. Had he not known G personally, he would have declared him dead at the scene, but instead, he ordered a life flight to Harborview Medical Center, which bought us 48 more hours with our son. Although the hemispheres of his brain were completely separated, his C1 and C2 dislocated, and his ocular nerves severed, sustaining at least 3 massive brain bleeds and numerous internal injuries, he NEVER looked more beautiful than when I kissed his face as he was being prepped for his flight to Harborview. Truly. G literally glowed with what I can only describe as bliss. Now, I understand that he had already gone to Heaven.

Somehow, miraculously, G bore the brunt of the crash and was the only one "seriously" injured out of the 5 vehicles. I later learned that he sustained enough damage to his brain to have killed every person involved. Given his self-sacrificing nature, we are sure he would not have it any other way and would not be able to live with himself if the roles were reversed. Please understand that I am not OK that my son died this way.

In case you are wondering, time does not heal all wounds. Time is NOT a healer; it's not capable of that. Time, in my opinion, is best described as a marinade. I will always remember how G kissed my cheek hard before eagerly running out the front door that night.

This is my 8th year and will be our 9th holiday season, with my last thought as I close my eyes, and my first thought in the morning is the distance between Heaven and Earth. While Gian feels like he might be just around the corner, memories of Harborview Brain Trauma Unit and the Brain Death Protocol invade many Fridays, Saturdays, and Sundays, with the sound of G's girlfriend wailing as she said goodbye. The image of my girls' faces pressed into their brother's hands, pleading for a miracle. Each holiday, every family gathering, and birthday, all weddings, each baby announcement, steel toe boots, trucks, meat products, intersections, stoplights, hard hats, all things with the letter G, every time I see his Dadio's jawline, the fact that both sisters eyes are turning from brown to green, every time someone asks how many children we have. This is why my chest hurts, and my throat constricts. This also explains the tattoos on my left arm, the reason we have a puppy, and the cause of our depression, anxiety, and Post Traumatic Stress Disorder. It's the reason I feel panic when my phone rings, how I lost a lot of hair, and became a lingering hugger.

Since Gian went Home, I now have a growing heart-shaped rock collection and essentially find heart shapes in clouds, crumbs, dirt clods, and everything everywhere. Every baby boy with blonde curls reminds me of Gian. This is why I find myself staring at young men, wishing I could hug them. It's the reason we moved. This is why I hold my breath. The reason I cry sometimes when I see sliced lunch meat. Why I don't care about things like politics, drama, disagreements, or flat tires. This is the reason I live every day just like it could be my last. My son taught me to do that.

Gian's life and death are the reasons I have become intimately acquainted with the difference between privilege and rights and that the

REPEATED THINGS WE DO AND THE CALCULATED RISKS WE TAKE CARRY CONSEQUENCES. COLLISIONS ARE THE RESULT OF CHOICES, NOT INTENTIONS. GIAN'S RIGHT TO LIFE, LIBERTY, AND THE PURSUIT OF HAPPINESS WAS CUT OFF BY SOMEONE ELSE'S PRIVILEGE.

DRIVING IS NOT A RIGHT.

I'VE BEEN 8YRS IN A MARINADE MS. M. CHOSE FOR US AND AM TRUSTING GIAN'S STORY ALONG WITH THE INFORMATION PRESENTED HERE, WILL HELP TO BRING CLARITY TO THE POWER OF OUR CHOICES. MY CHOICES, YOUR CHOICES, OUR CHOICES.

I FORGAVE HER AS WE DROVE THROUGH THE CRASH SITE, AND I CONTINUE TO FORGIVE HER EACH DAY. I PRAY HER LIFE IS ONLY SWEETER, HER CHOICES ARE MUCH MORE INTENTIONAL, AND THAT SHE UNDERSTANDS THE GIFT SHE HAS BEEN GRANTED TO BE PART OF HER OWN CHILDREN'S LIVES. I AM SO GRATEFUL EACH OF US, EACH OF YOU, IS ALIVE AND ABLE TO BE HERE TODAY TO CONTINUE LEARNING AND CHOOSING HOW WE WANT TO AFFECT THE WORLD AROUND US.

GIAN LIVED WELL BECAUSE HE CHOSE TO. PLEASE CHOOSE WELL.

BEFORE I SAY GOODBYE, [I SAY TO THE CROWD] THERE ARE A FEW THOUGHTS ON MY HEART SPECIFICALLY FOR YOU THIS EVENING.

YOU'VE BEEN EXPOSED TO SOME HEAVY, DEEPLY IMPORTANT INFORMATION THIS EVENING. ALL OF THIS IS FOR YOU. WE ARE HERE TONIGHT, SHARING TONIGHT BECAUSE WE CARE ABOUT YOU. THIS EFFORT IS FUELED BY OUR HOPE AND OUR LOVE FOR YOU, FOR YOUR LOVED ONES, FOR YOUR FUTURE. WE DON'T HAVE TO KNOW YOU TO LOVE YOU. THAT FACT BECAME BLAZINGLY CLEAR TO ME AS THE LIFE SUPPORT MACHINES WERE TURNED OFF AND AS GIAN WENT HOME.

My heart has been cracked wide open in the best way.

You matter, and the way you choose to live matters. All of it--not just some of how you do life, all of how you do life matters. The big and the little things really matter. The things out loud and the things no one else sees. We'll never know the impact of all the big and little choices until we leave. As hard or as easy as it has been for you to get to this evening, whatever challenges you're facing, things you've overcome, or whatever you are going through right now, today is a gift not everyone has been given.

That we are here together is a massive gift. Maybe even a miracle.

Remember this moment. Remember this breath. Remember these people here giving their time, knowledge, and stories. It's all a gift.

We only come this way once. We don't get to do this one moment again.

When Gian told me he wanted to do something important with his life, that he was going to take the grenade for some people, did he have you in mind? Probably. It's amazing to me that when he said, "There's no greater love than to lay down your life for one's friends," that he was referring to you now 8yrs later, in this gathering in a state he had never been to. But Gian was like that. He made friends everywhere he went.

Gian built a legacy in his 18yrs. In his simple, clear coming and going. So are you.

So am I.

So, I want to ask you, who is "that guy" to you? Who is that precious, golden person to you? Maybe you are that guy, that girl. Maybe you're not that person yet, but you want to be. Please choose to be. The world didn't have enough time with Gian or his way of showing up, but you're here, and the world desperately needs you to show up beautifully, thoughtfully, generously, bravely, and kindly. Please be intentional with your one life.

Ms. M. will live with the fact that she contributed to Gian's death. What do you want to live with?

She carries that into her future. So do her children. What do you want to carry into your future? Into your own family's future?

Gian lived intentionally and quite unusually for a person his age. How do you want to be remembered?

His choices, the way he worked to really see people and, along with his care, impacted the people around him in astonishing ways. What do you want your impact to be?

Lastly, legacy is partially defined as anything handed down from the past, as from an ancestor or predecessor. I would like to pass Gian's legacy on to you like a baton. Please take it and run.

Thank you for listening. Choose well. I love you."

To be clear, Ms. M. is not my enemy. Death is. She just partnered with it.

G's JOURNAL

"It's better to die on your feet than live on your knees."
Emiliano Zapata

Gian writes,

"...I will die doing what others dream impossible, absurd, and horrendous. I will die doing what others are afraid to do."

This statement was in response to a writing prompt in G's senior year of high school. He was just seventeen years old when he wrote that. I discovered so much about our boy within the pages of that precious baby blue, sparkly, spiral-bound notebook. He tasked his little sister to pick out his writing journal. She laughed and laughed as she contemplated the cover options at the store. She could have chosen a kitten-themed cover, camouflage, or the basic solid red. When Zosia presented her brother with her selection for him, he didn't even blink. He just said, "Perfect!" and tucked the journal into his pack and moved on to the next thing. She didn't get the rise out of him she was hoping for that time.

Of all the famous quotes available to describe himself, he selected Emiliano Zapata's. G and I are very different people. I worked hard, passionately, to keep him alive, healthy, happy, and growing while he devoted himself to learning how to give his life away.

Hindsight is 20/20, as the saying goes, AND I look forward to the day that I have an inkling of the impact that belongs to our tenderhearted and princely warrior. I cannot help but marvel at

G's clarity, the fulfillment of his heart's design, and the accomplishment of his deepest desire.

As my family's understanding was opening up to what our new reality meant and as we grappled to live it, we began to crave and thirst for a justice that our world could not satisfy us with, so God gave me a dream to share from His heavenly perspective.

Finding the Gold

Who are the golden ones in your life, and why? What legacy are you handing to your loved ones? Are you satisfied? What are you fighting for, and how? What have you gained in all that you've lost?

ELEVEN

Finally, A Dream!

"I'VE CASHED IN MY INVESTMENT." FATHER GOD

Sometimes our minds get offended as He goes after our hearts.
~ Alanna

Finally, a DREAM! I never imagined God's version of justice would come packaged this way. In the midst of the mess, along with our invitation to begin to push back on the darkness that threatened to take us over, God gifted me His Heavenly perspective with a sweet dose of Gian's ongoing life away from planet Earth.

My Journal entry, June 9, 2018

It's easy to see the gold in dreams like this:

... ♡♡♡...June 3rd, night after Gian's 21st birthday, I had a dream. Finally, a dream!

Gian and I were facing each other with a wide railing of some kind between us. We were leaning in, talking, and I noticed a bit of roast beef (maybe?) in his teeth. Here's the thing: I knew he had gone to Heaven, and yet our visit was in real-time. I asked from pure curiosity, "Oh, did you have roast beef for lunch?" G said, "Mom! We've talked and decided to be friends." I recognized a hint of something in his voice, not sadness necessarily and he did not indicate a specific person. He spoke these words while handing me what appeared to be a high-quality, very masculine wristwatch that was buckled with a few things (rings?) secured somehow in the buckle. When his hands left the watch, I looked up, and he was gone.

What I remember next is standing in a grassy gathering area facing a tall stone wall. I didn't see the top of it. This time, in my hands, were some documents with a long horizontal photo clipped on top. As I looked at the picture, I realized it was taken from the place I was standing, having captured an event I am so grateful to have in my memory. Even if only a dream!

In the picture, I see three or more men with shoulder-length hair, very muscular shoulders, and arms facing Gian's back. They are smiling, watching, leaning forward. Gian is receiving a deep elbow handshake from another muscular armed man. Only this one has a helmet on that covers his face. I know he's a centurion. Somehow, I know. Gian is smiling with closed lips. I see he is humbled and accepting whatever is happening. He's pleased. There are wisps of smoke in the picture.

Then I woke up. Within a few minutes, I shared with Jeff and decided to write down all I could recall quickly. As I paused to focus on what I remembered from my dream, the picture that was in my hands at the stone wall came to mind. As I sat there on the couch wide awake, the picture became a scene that played out in front of me:

and I watched as Gian was united with a beautiful brotherhood that was eager to have him. They had waited for him! The wisps of smoke floating by as I watched my son join his people.

Actually, as I thought *brotherhood*, I was interrupted with *mighty men of valor.*[i]

Then they were gone together.

GIAN DIDN'T LEAVE ALONE. HE ISN'T ALONE! HE'S LIVING out his destiny with his people ♡♡♡...clearly, there's so much I don't understand. As I have continued to ponder this dream, the wristwatch comes to mind. I don't believe Gian was talking about a person when he said, "We've talked and decided to be friends." I think he was talking about time. He lives outside the limits or constraints of time now. I believe the rings that I had a glimpse of are the commitments he made and the relationships he created. These commitments and relationships are not limited to people and are no longer held by time either, as love and people are eternal. I am deeply curious about what all of this means and am eager to know and understand all that Heaven holds for me.

I've only had three dreams of Gian that I can recall, the third one being the one I just shared. I am envious of the prolific dream lives of some of my friends who have children in Heaven. Dreams can be a way for God to communicate with us, and I want more of that!

The very first dream I remember having just the next morning after returning home from Harborview,

Gian appeared to me wearing camouflage pants and a red plaid flannel shirt. Ha! He seemed carefree but leaned in close and said, "I'm making you sad."

I replied, "No, this makes me sad."

As he disappeared from my sight, I awoke.

The second dream came a few mornings later. In the early dawn, I saw Gian with his arms resting at his sides, being lifted up above the ground when suddenly a shower of gold coins flew out from behind him and fell downward toward me with almost violent force. As I opened my eyes, I heard the words, "I've cashed in My investment."

Initially, I was offended by the gold coins and the phrase because I only wanted my son. So, I placed the dream *on the shelf* of my heart for safekeeping, much like the other mysteries of my life. Yet even while *on the shelf*, I recognized how this encounter revealed the way God esteems Gian as precious, sees him as highly valued, and pure like gold.

Somehow, the gold of Gian's life was released, or maybe changed possession as he went Home.

Recently, the Lord reminded me again of the gold coin dream just minutes before He opened up my understanding. In my remembering, I was thanking God for His incredible love for Gian, for valuing his life enough to associate him with gold, for allowing me to invest Gian's story in the world, as He had invested in me with the gift of a son...and now I get it—sort of.

Jesus told a parable in Luke nineteen, beginning with verse twelve,[ii] about a nobleman who gave his servants gold coins with instruction to engage in business or invest them while he was away receiving a kingdom. Upon the nobleman's return, he asked his servants what they had gained with HIS coins, with HIS gold... Father God is waiting, watching to see what I will do with His gold coins, the gold of His Gian's life. G isn't mine alone. He always belonged to Him too. The gold that has been so graciously, generously handed to me has a heavenly demand on it. The gold is to be multiplied, not kept isolated, warm in a pocket, or quite literally covered with a dirt clod out of fear.

What an honor to be entrusted with something so costly, precious, and eternal. I want "well done, good and faithful servant"[iii] to be the declaration that shines through my life.

While the gold coin dream didn't initially feel good, the Lord expounded on it as I chose to come out of my initial offense and be curious about what it all meant. Sometimes, our minds get offended as He goes after our hearts. Hearts and heads speak different languages.

We are far more valuable than our minds can comprehend, and we can wrestle trying to understand what is outside of human reason. But our hearts understand completely. All the gold on the planet would never be enough to balance my love for my children, and the gold that rained down on me in the dream wasn't from Earth. It came from Heaven.

While it's true that some things have changed, it's more accurate to say that a lot of things remain the same.

It is absolutely true that Gian is living out his destiny uninhibited by earthly limitations, pain-free, and full of joy. He has no concern or worry for the world or his loved ones, as each and every issue on Earth is already solved in Heaven. He lives IN the solution, full of confidence. Regardless of Gian's whereabouts, I miss him even if he is in Heaven. I still want to be included in his life, and I want updates, photos of the latest adventure, and a play-by-play of how the big battle went down. I want him to tell me his perspective on current events, and I want to sit close enough to him to smell his cologne. I want to know about what's happening in his heart, and I want to thank him to his face for sharing his light grey Carhartt sweatshirt with me this morning. The wants don't just stop when our loved ones go Home.

Dreams like the first one I shared point to the higher reality that is now part of my relationship with Gian. While I am thrilled he doesn't have to navigate the current political and social atmosphere or more heartbreak or financial strain as a young man, I am missing his presence in a world that would really benefit from another good man. Specifically, I miss his presence in my world. We raised him to love and honor God and people, and I am SO grateful he had that part of his life figured out early, as well as his sisters, who are missing his leadership and guidance as big brother, his bear hugs, and protection. Important people don't just suddenly stop being important.

Until we get to be with him again and meet that band of brothers, those *mighty men of valor*, we're going to be uncomfortable with the perceived distance between Heaven and Earth. I *know* that it's really just a thin veil, but that veil feels immense to me most moments.

Finding the Gold

We all have gold to do something with. Is your gold a person? Persons? A message? A talent or gifting? Is your gold literal gold? How are you investing the gold Heaven has given you?

TWELVE

Making Every Moment Matter

JUST LOVE THE ONE IN FRONT OF YOU

Invest your precious heartbeats well.
~ Anonymous

We **only come this way once.** I had no idea just how accurate that statement was until Gian left. It's as if Gian said, "I'm going to live a really good life so you can tell my beautiful story."

Gian may have been in kindergarten when he brought home a bracelet to give to his Dadio, with the words "Make Every Moment Matter" inscribed on it. Jeff wore the bracelet faithfully for years until it finally fell off on its own. I remember the initial impact the word "matter" made on me as I contemplated the phrase in comparison to the all-familiar and similar yet nearly polar opposite (in implication) phrase, "Make every moment count."

Jeff and I let this phrase impact how we raised our kids and then how we worked to stay connected to our teenagers and now our adult daughters. The heartbeat behind that message is how I am *raising* myself. Reminding myself over and over again to "just love the one in front of you" is an encouragement to keep at "making every moment matter."

From the time G was just a little guy, he had been generally quick to offer his help. We have a photo of him, when he was just four years old, pushing a child-sized wheelbarrow with a load of yard gravel from a work party he attended with my Mom. He worked hard with the adults all day, moving load after load of rocks. The owner of the home was so overwhelmed by his work ethic she gifted him a Costco-sized jug of Jellybellys™! He was so proud and happily shared his reward with us when he got home.

Even as he got older, there were really only a few eye-rolls when my requests for his assistance interrupted something important to him. He seemed to *get* the significance of his presence and the way he could *help* in even mundane tasks. While his sisters and I never shied away from heavy work, he was often the heavy lifter when his Dad wasn't home. Commonly, the heavy lifting involved them working together, side by side. I loved watching them work together. Sweating together is so much better than sweating alone. Over and over, he chose to invest his presence, strength, kindness, silliness, friendship, generosity, encouragement, and protection liberally. His desire to do something really important with his life was obvious, as he didn't waste any time loving the one in front of him. Looking back, I am in awe of the wisdom that Gian allowed to direct his life.

There's a lot in this life, in motherhood with my three gems, and specific to my treasured memories with G, that I am deeply, bedrock-bottom-of-my-heart type grateful for.

That Gian was able to identify the importance of his minutes, hours, and days is thought-provoking. I am so grateful that he was somehow able to discern his days on the planet were short and, from that strange awareness, chose to make a difference by living for the benefit of those around him. I am deeply grateful that he understood that he would only come this way once, and I am working on that myself.

Looking back, he seemed to know that his today would never happen again. Maybe even that they were short. His grasping of the understanding that not one of his heartbeats would ever be repeated or even multiplied is astounding. He lived with no idea of what tomorrow or the next 10 minutes held for him or for any of us, and yet he lived so fully and intentionally.

He seemed to easily look for and identify the gold in the people around him and was aware that it takes no skill to see the dirt on people. Dirt is often so obvious.

Who could he be a friend to? Who could he comfort? Who could he encourage? Who could he sit next to? Who was hungry? Who could he pray for? Who could he help?

We later found out he was busy doing just that. He had comforted and befriended a girl he found crying in the upstairs hallway at school. She later shared her story at Gian's candlelight vigil held at the same high school. Dozens of people spoke that night about the way Gian made them feel and why they loved him. One boy (now a full-grown man serving in the Marine Corps) told us that Gian treated him like a big brother would, and for the first time, he felt like he belonged somewhere. Gian had hopes of becoming a Marine and had several conversations with the Marine Corps Recruiters about enlisting. I imagine he is so proud of his *little brother* for doing the brave thing. If I had it to do over, I would have encouraged Gian to follow his heart. Maybe he'd still be here.

It was at this same event that we learned about how G always gave one of his sandwiches away. Suddenly, it made sense to me why one of his sammies had to be made a certain way and was different from the other two.

He looked for ways to help. As I shared in the statement prepared for the MADD events, the only time he got suspended was when he stuck up for one of his favorite teachers while in high school. We know that Ms. K. was always more than capable of protecting herself, but when another student became openly and aggressively disrespectful toward her, Gian intervened. G confronted the young man by telling him he needed to stop talking to her that way. Because the behavior didn't stop, G got closer to him, repeating the direction to stop. One of G's buddies stepped in to grab G by the shoulders, which caused his body to lurch forward, resulting in a forceful chest bump. The other boy's parent called the school to complain, hence the suspension. Ms. K still refers to Gian as her "hero." More than a few times, she bought him steaks as a thank-you for his help in the classroom.

This kind of care continued into his workplace as he defended a man who G thought to be in his 40s. While the bullying was only verbal, I asked Gian if he felt fear while defending this man to his coworkers, and he replied, "No, I know I'm never alone." He told me there were times he could see his angels. His bravery still made me nervous, even if angels were present.

To make something count, there's a score or a tally being kept, an end goal, a competition, something to be accomplished. Maybe someone wins. Definitely transactional.

How do we make our finite moments significant? To make anything, including a second of our lives, impactful is subjective, personal, and relational. What compels me to action is weighed in my heart and could be vastly different than what motivates you. When we're focusing on what really matters or making a connection, investment, quality, closeness, or a moment matter, the goal is not keeping score.

Similarly, emphasizing quality over quantity means being aware of the investment potential in the people we are gifted with and how we choose to engage them. For instance, as we desire quality time with our favorite people, we often need an enormous quantity of time for quality time to occur. Yet, it's just a handful (if we're lucky) of rich connections that impact us so significantly and stay with us for our lifetime. Investing is risky as well because we may not see a return in our lifetime.

All we have is right now.

If I knew my days with Gian would be short, I would have done nearly everything differently. I would have ended all multi-tasking when my children were present. I would have stopped everything as one of them spoke to me to make eye contact and listen with my whole self. I would always laugh at their jokes, eat whatever they prepared for me, and dance with them in the kitchen and the grocery store aisles. I would go back and sing out loud with them, and I would have cried with them when they cried instead of trying to fix their problems, only to cry later by myself. I would listen with my heart more and with my head less.

> *If anything matters, then everything matters. Because you are important, everything you do is important. Every time you forgive, the universe changes; every time you reach out and touch a heart or a life, the world changes; with every kindness and service, seen or unseen, God's purposes are accomplished, and nothing will ever be the same again.*
>
> — THE SHACK BY WILLIAM PAUL YOUNG

We only have this minute, just this breath and this heartbeat. Make it significant for you and the one in front of you. Make it a moment neither of you will forget.

My Facebook post, June 22, 2022

> *In case no one has told you, YOU are irreplaceable. Irreplaceable. No one else has your voice or exact thought patterns; no one matches the lift and fall of your laughter. I dare say that no one can step in and hug the way you do. Sure, someone else may be able to offer a similar skill set for employment purposes or as a teammate, but as a Momma, I can tell you with absolute certainty that you are the only* ***you*** *there is.*

I HAVE LOOKED HIGH AND LOW FOR THE BEAUTIFUL young man who could compare to my Gian. There are many, many good men on the planet, and I am so grateful to know several of them, yet my search has been to no avail. Two of G's good friends have made similar statements about trying to establish friendships since G went home. While they have finally added new friends to their circles, still no one compares to G.

Just as there is no one that compares to Gian, no one compares to *you*. Just as his place with us is for him alone, your place is for you alone. This reality is true for each of us. No one can fill the place that is you on the planet or in Heaven. This is precisely why our moments are so precious, why we CAN make them matter. It's because we are in them.

Finding the Gold

What are you giving your precious time, energy heart beats, and attention to? Because you matter, how are you caring for your own heart?

THIRTEEN

Surviving To Thriving

CLARIFICATIONS ON GRIEF, LOSS, AND TRAUMA

Vilomah.
~ Sanskrit word that translates into "against a natural order."
This word is offered to bereaved parents, similar to widow or widower.

Time heals all wounds is a common phrase coined by the Greek poet Menander around 300 B.C..[i] Time certainly has its place in the process of recovering or acclimating to significant change, wounding, loss, and healing from grief and trauma. "New normal" is a term I was introduced to, and I may have gagged on when I first heard it. The death of a child violates the laws of nature and the order of life, which brings with it a dynamic that I would never wish on my worst enemy. The story I tell myself is even our worst enemies have respect for children—except death. Death has no respect for any of us.

Time in itself has no ability to heal, though. Time is neutral. As I've shared before, to me, time is like a marinade. Just like steak in a marinade takes time, and with time and the influence of the spices, herbs, and sauces, the steak changes. The meat's texture and flavor are influenced by all of it. So, *we* also take on the flavor of whatever we are soaking in, whatever we are repeatedly exposed to. More time, more marinating in pain, trauma, or victimization does not equate to healing. That's not possible. Time or marinating in pain that is unaddressed can cause bitterness and callousness, increase our physical and mental pain, doubt, hopelessness, and physical illness if we aren't intentional in regard to our thought life and how we manage our hearts and our souls. This is especially crucial as moments become days, and days become weeks, and months and years. The body really does keep the score, but it's not designed to harbor the harm we have endured.

Our friends, our family, and complete strangers showed up for us as unconditional love. They lavished us with their kindness, faith, love, tears, encouragement, healing prayers, honesty, patience—EXTREME patience—support, and care to enrich our marinade. Unconditional love influences the impact of time, and it provides the conduit for healing, wholeness, and thriving to emerge organically and as mourning or grieving is worked through our lives. Just as tears are intended to come out and not be held back, mourning, grief, and trauma are meant to be faced and worked on so all of it can be worked out of our souls and fully out of our bodies and our whole being. To be clear, I don't know if I will ever finish the work of mourning the loss of our Gian. I miss him every day, and I suspect the aroma of his life, combined with my love for him, will impact me and my presence in the world until I'm with him again.

Every morning presents an opportunity to continue facing what I'm experiencing and deciding where I'm going to turn for the truth and for comfort.

Unconditional Love swooped in, and He wrapped strong arms around us right in the middle of the horribly-horrible to sustain us, as our physical bodies had to work hard to walk through shock and trauma, and His name was Jesus. I undeniably felt the unconditional love of God in every human hug and in every bit of kindness. I saw the unconditional love of our good God in each friendly smile and in the patience of listening to friends and family. Unconditional Love hasn't let go of us and certainly hasn't finished its or His work in us.

Just a few weeks after the crash, I was sitting at the pass-through at our old house; the pass-through was a piece of a retired bowling alley lane that we repurposed and one of the best improvements we made while living there.

As I glanced up to look into the living area, I caught sight of a shadow shimmer of Gian. As he stood there smiling, I could suddenly *see* all the things he had smiled through.

He smiled through knee, elbow, hip, and shoulder injuries. He smiled through heartbreaks from friends and life circumstances while experiencing personal injustices and those that occurred around him. He smiled through discouragement, rejection, and harshness. Suddenly, I could *see* what he had smiled through for such a long time...and then I *saw* as the blunt force of the collision hit his body, he was instantly in the arms of his Father, and I heard Him say with such force,

> *I know it all! I know every bit of it! I got you! I love you! You're home now!*

Life is MANY things. Life is beautiful, hard, brutal, ugly, fruitful, innocent, complicated, unfair, challenging, promising, invigorating...and eternal.

It's very strange to admit, but our lives have improved as we've suffered, and in some massive ways since the crash. It's easy for me to be offended by my own realization, but this is part of the thriving possibility. This is part of looking for the gold, for massive good to come of our loss, and for beauty to come from my ashes. Thriving is never guaranteed, even for a life that's untouched by devastation, and I'm not even sure I remember how the concept of thriving out of heartsmash occurred to me. Maybe I dreamt it because it was dream-worthy! I NEVER would have imagined being able to say that I could begin to thrive out of heartsmash. There's just grace for it.

And it sounds grotesque, doesn't it?! How can the worst, nightmarish thing that happens to your child, to you, to your loved ones somehow usher in goodness? Only by the sheer grace of God, ONLY. And sometimes, the details need to be worked out a sliver, and then a facet at a time, because He wants to highlight our importance and our significance in the process to finally reveal the gem that's been there all along. There is beauty. There is gold. Training myself to look for it, to be willing to look for it, and then to begin to expect it has been like having water wings on in the expansive sea of loss. When I get tired, those little things help to keep my nose above the water line. I am emphatically NOT saying the crash made us better. I am saying that God's goodness entered our lives as a direct response to it.

ONLY by the grace of God.

It's as if Gian is shoulder to shoulder with the Messiah, leaning over the windows of Heaven, pointing us out to Him because *nothing is wasted* or outside of His goodness, saying something like, "Let's get 'em, real good. Let's show them that EVERYTHING can be golden as they lean into Heaven and pursue You.

Let's help them remember they are only passing through. Remind them to keep giving You their ashes and that You'll make everything beautiful and golden. You'll make them beautiful!"

Early on and as the days became weeks, I experienced increasing physical symptoms that I was desperate to have relief from. Alarming, sudden, sharp pain would shoot through my chest, into my arms, radiating into my throat and jaw. During these intense moments, I found it nearly impossible to talk, think, or finish swallowing the food that was sometimes still in my esophagus. The lump that would form in my throat during those times would lock my entire throat closed. I found that a sip (or a few glasses) of wine would all but completely stop the progression of this experience if I could meet the shooting pain within a second or two. You can probably imagine the new challenge I began to face—wine is not a savior, although it can be medicinal and enjoyable—until it's not. Wine or anything else can easily evolve into something other than how it introduced itself, especially when pain or trauma is involved. Eventually, the wild shooting pain lessened and mostly stopped, but by then, I was in the habit of preventing physical pain by proactively having 2 or more glasses of wine as soon as I was home from work. While 2 or 3 glasses of wine may not be heavy drinking compared to some, it's really not about the volume; it is about what I would continue to invite into my life that would impact me and my loved ones.

Over and over, *I get to choose* to set down and lay down what isn't helping anymore.

Any excesses...work, chocolate, social media, wine, attempting to control outcomes, avoidance, staying angry.

While it is true that distracting and/or medicating ourselves can be very helpful for a time, it's also accurate to say that both can eventually interfere with healing and ultimately thriving. I've learned that when I am quick to reach for something to soothe or to distract, it's because I have a real need that is waiting to be met. Often, I am mentally and emotionally tired at the end of the day, and I don't really need a glass of wine to ease my frayed nerves; maybe I need to laugh or just need to put myself to bed. I know it's time to adjust how I'm doing things when I wake in the morning and recognize the presence of regret, with my first thought having to do with skipping chocolate or wine today. My conscience and Holy Spirit want to help me face what's hurting me (and you), to set down the things that temporarily medicate but ultimately intend to control and limit our future. A life of freedom, wholeness, and thriving are just on the other side of what we lay down. Our souls are screaming for kindness and care. I am still learning how to sit with the things that hurt my heart, my mind, and sometimes my body, and sometimes take my breath away. Feeling what we feel can be exhausting, scary, eye-opening, and incredibly helpful.

As I've discussed, Unconditional Love has shown up tangibly for me in the form of friends, family, a counselor or two, coworkers, strangers, songs on the radio, puppy cuddles and wiggles, heart-shaped rocks, sunshine in my face, those living room floor moments when Jesus steps in, and the sudden peace that washes over me. There's never any harshness when unconditional love shows up for me, and always there's honesty. Unconditional Love invites us fully into and through grief, mourning, trauma, and survival mindsets moment by moment and as we begin to look up again. The key is to take those (often baby) steps out of what's held us as those steps present themselves. Smiling, laughing, and hugging are big, powerful gestures that lead to thriving.

Thriving isn't accidental work, and it's a good, mature adult *thing* to ask for help when we need it and sometimes when we don't think we do, but others ask us to. Getting professional help has been and will continue to be part of our wholeness journey, too. While we haven't successfully connected with a licensed therapist for ongoing support in a few years, early on, Dadio and I did have several eye movement desensitization and reprocessing therapy (EMDR) treatments that were very helpful to us individually, and ultimately helpful to us as a family.[ii]

EMDR is a mental health treatment technique that is used to treat Post-Traumatic Stress Disorder and other mental health issues. The method involves eye movement while processing a memory or event.

The particular doctor who administered the treatments did not require a lot of talk for (or much language at all) the EMDR to do what it does. Not relying heavily on *talk therapy* was especially helpful as we often didn't have the right words, or any words for that matter, to express any part of what was happening inside us.

Sometimes, the words were too ugly to say out loud. We just needed to be able to function better and to feel more stable inside of our own skin. Dadio went from fear and dread, knowing he would have to drive through the same intersection, to then throwing up every time he drove through it, and for him, that was a handful of times each work day. These days and nights became pure torture, just anticipating his drive to work. After a few EMDR sessions, Jeff was able to drive through the intersection, being fully aware of what happened there, but was no longer vomiting or feeling terrorized by his heartbreak in the same way. This doctor explained that the therapy doesn't fix anything; it just helps to support us while we endure it.

Thankfully, the effects of trauma and complicated grief are more understood than they have ever been, with several strong supporting therapies available.

We all need someone, and we all need help sometimes. Probably multiple someones, and at multiple times, actually. My heart of hearts tells me that I need a Heavenly Counselor, and I feel my spirit drink in Heavenly truth that flows from the books I read, conversations with heart and spirit-driven friends and teachers (lots of my family are my friends, too), and prayer. Connection and accountability can be present in many forms, and I've relied on all of them heavily in my life.

Although I am a wallflower who prefers hearing about someone else's life to sharing my own story, connecting with people who understand or are willing to try to understand has become like oxygen. My first recognition of understanding that it is like oxygen to my body happened as Liza, Jackson's mom, came into G's hospital room and sat down. She arrived with her sister Tina, who was Gian and his sister GB's favorite elementary teacher. Liza's son went home just a year and a half before Gian, and as she took the chair near the foot of his hospital bed, I felt like I was in the presence of a saint or an angel. My physical self immediately became calm. Maybe because she carries some heaven with her, too. There's an unmistakable and often instant bond between parents who lose a child. Although we may differ on many things, as most humans on the planet who use their own brains do, we have, in my humble opinion, the most important linking aspects in complete agreement. Life is precious. Uncertain. Risky. Sometimes, it's too short. Love your people while you have the chance and find your tribe. I breathe easier in these precious one's presence.

Tribe is a rich word, isn't it? The shape and size of our tribe have shifted over the years, and my favorite aspect of ours is that regardless of the time that passes between our hugs, our love for each other is upfront and allows us to pick up where we left off. Mommas that have buried their children are my people. Dadios that have loved their babies beyond the grave are my favorite men on the planet. And our precious friends and family members who chose to get closer as Gian's machines were turned off, and since—goodness—these are walking treasures. Not everyone gets the privilege of walking someone all the way Home and when we get to do that as a community, it's supernatural. There's no way to get out of that experience untouched.

One of those who chose to get closer introduced us to massage therapy, which proved to be one of the kindest and most helpful forms of medicine that we could add to our lives. Our bodies quickly began to let us know that they were processing what our hearts and minds were struggling with. Just as we weren't sure anymore how much ibuprofen we should be regularly taking to manage our very real physical pain, a friend from high school reached out and brought us into her practice. Angela provided such intuitive, kind, prayerful care, and our bodies began to relax, rest, and recover. Our hearts, our minds, and our bodies had carried us through life pretty seamlessly for a long time. The care and love we began to show ourselves really should have been happening all along.

Prior to the crash, I was *grid-less*. I had zero grid for how each and every life event of each and every person in the world around me could and would potentially impact me in such a dramatic way. "Hurting people, hurt people" is a true statement, and I really didn't want to do that, while I immediately recognized that I could, in fact, take out a whole city block with the fire that was attempting to consume me if I wasn't careful. I felt apocalyptic. Still do some moments. It's not a good place to be and certainly not a place to take up residence. It's vitally important to be honest about what's happening in our inner world, and it is just as important to allow the heavenly-inspired shifts to occur that will potentially save our own souls and the relationships that mean the most to us from the potential destruction that inferno could cause. Marriages, friendships, and family connections don't always survive the death of a child. It's more common for them to not. The statistics are not encouraging.

Within just a few months, it became obvious that there were layers to the hurt/loss emerging, and managing my own heart would become a high priority. There were times when it was best to go silent as an honest response instead of trying to string words together that wouldn't violate my heart or hurt someone else. Silence can be honest, though, too, and just as powerful as any thoughtfully planned statement or response. Choosing my influence on the world around me meant I would need to carefully choose my words and constantly evaluate why I was or was not choosing to speak. Words create worlds, as the saying goes, and I did not and still do not want to hold people captive or destroy a relationship because of what might come out of my mouth during a painful moment.

Inner turmoil was a justified and understandable experience, following losing Gian, and this side of Heaven from an earthly perspective, the turmoil would never be sustainable. Interesting, isn't it? That which is justifiable can also destroy my life from the inside out.

The literal hellfire that was burning in my soul had to be extinguished for my own sanity, for the sake of my loved ones, and for my physical well-being. At a minimum, I had to choose to allow the kindness of others to help alter the fuel of the flames. Stoking those flames with hatred, anger, and persevering thoughts wouldn't make me more powerful and safer and would never influence my loved ones in the way that I have wanted from the very beginning. I've only ever wanted to be a representative of the love of God, kind of like a room diffuser. I want the aroma that I give off to perfume each room with God's love.

So, I've had to fight sliding into a bleak, black pit of despair with nearly every FB and Instagram post I scroll past, every blessing highlighted by even an acquaintance, like engagement announcements of Gian's friends, babies delivered, birthday celebrations with complaints about getting older, each time our girls were left out of gatherings or celebrations after the crash because they had suddenly become *party poopers*, and every birthday of Gian's when the world didn't stop on its axis to acknowledge that we have successfully traversed another year apart from him. The list doesn't end here, but this is where I'll stop.

For a long time, every good thing happening around me served to reveal both another layer of our *loss and an invitation* to celebrate the beauty still happening on the earth. The layers of our loss exposed us to incredible tenderness, and we often felt like life itself was being ripped off of us, revealing more of the bloody mess that wasn't healing fast enough. Every day seemed another opportunity to grieve yet another aspect of our loss while simultaneously presenting us with an invitation to celebrate the beauty of life. These layers of grief, loss, and celebration would become like fluorescent flashing targets for offense, comparison, blessing, compassion, and joy. Too much of my thought life would be wasted on the stories I've told myself about the lives behind the perfect and sparkly Facebook posts of people I love very much. Then I remind myself that most of us only post the pretty parts of our lives. Those frame-worthy moments are so easy to highlight and thoroughly worthy of celebrating. I do, with all my heart, believe that what we focus on and what we celebrate increases in our lives. Each time I chose to acknowledge the blessing, the good, the gold—the celebration occurring in someone else's life, I could feel my heart expand even in its devastation. My heart would ache as in a stretch to hold both my own pain and my joy for another human being.

I recognized my desire for people to make me OK by including me and my family and by remembering Gian and all the other fine details of every big and teeny tiny silly and impossible thing that was only known by me. I realized I had unmet expectations of my friends and family (of the world) when my disappointment showed up, as I realized I hadn't been invited to another *Mom's* outing or that Gian wasn't remembered in the right way. Ridiculous! I feel the slippery slope and the invitation open to despair when my eyes stay too long on the temporal and on comparison.

When I adjust what I lean into and turn my focus toward Heaven, to Home—everything changes. Everything becomes clear. Every time I bring my heartsmash, bleakness, despair, sorrow, anger, confusion, jealousy, my need to be affirmed, and my ashes to God, He turns it around in me. Somehow and miraculously, He turns what I'm experiencing around until I have peace and assurance and *see* the beauty He is creating in and through our ashes and our highlights. As I let my expectations go, sure enough, someone reaches out to let me know they *remember*.

Just as it was easy, so very easy for me to thank God that Ms. M got to leave the hospital and go home with her son, while I did not, I have chosen to let myself celebrate what is going well for the world around me, even when my own life hasn't gone well in the same way. I chose to let my heart cheer through tears as Gian's sweetheart was finally able to date again, become engaged, and see pictures of her wedding, while Gian didn't get those things. Even while my heart aches, I find it celebrating naturally. There is a both/and. What we focus on increases.

There are celebration-worthy events happening all around me, and I want those doors of joy and celebration in my heart to stay open! I want my heart to literally be a wide-open place for celebration. Bleak, black despair is not for humans, and celebrating what can be celebrated has buoyed my heart and mind. I want to be one of the first people my friends come to to share their beautiful news! I want the opportunity to acknowledge the hard-fought victories, the promotions, the cash windfalls, the surprise baby, the restored relationship, the answered prayer, the miraculous healing, the heavenly provision, and angelic visitation or protection because Psalm 27:13[iii] says I can, I want to experience the goodness of God in the land of the living for me and for everyone beyond my sight.

So, thinking about what I'm thinking about has become kind of a full-time job that I'm checking in with all day long. In those moments that I recognize my thoughts are spiraling around topics that lead to depression or anxiety, I pause to acknowledge the swirl and then say out loud, "No. I don't receive that." I follow my statement by turning my focus to all that is going well inside the moment I find myself in.

You cannot keep birds from flying over your head,
but you can keep them from building a nest.[iv]

— MARTIN LUTHER

So it is with our thought lives.

As a young mom, I was introduced to the concept of thinking about what I'm thinking about. A key to that concept is that not all thoughts are worthy of our time and headspace, are accurate, helpful, peaceful, or lead us in a healthy direction. This guidance was particularly helpful during the span of years that it took to wrap up the legal aspect of the crash; my thought-life felt like an active battleground with bombs going off as I would go grocery shopping, attempt to read, or close my eyes to sleep. I had the option not to be involved or be made aware of the details and developments; however, for Gian to be made relevant in the proceedings, we had to be there, which meant we would have to wrestle with some information in our hearts and minds.

To say we were exhausted and desperately clinging to hope would be accurate. These details produced thoughts, ideas, and mindsets that would eventually have to confront the heart of God for us and for Gian. Nearly all of it would be deemed unworthy of God's presence. Not because it didn't matter but because everything pertaining to Gian is precious in His sight, and the accusations coming against Gian's value were lies. According to God's heart, there was nothing to worry about and nothing to prove. He encouraged me to let it all out and tell Him all my hopes, fears, disappointments, and the worst-case scenarios I created in my mind and then look up to Him. He also taught me to anticipate and watch for His intervention. He asked me over and over to look to Him, to trust Him and His version of justice, and assured me that justice was coming. Over and over and over, and at every wakeup and with every good night, I would bring my mind back to all that is true, honest, just, pure, lovely, the things of good report, all that is virtuous and praiseworthy. Slowly, my mind began to naturally recognize, return to, and dwell on all that was well. Eight years later, there are still moments, hours, and even days that my mind needs extra coaxing and leading to focus Heavenward.

I've determined to continue to take the time to think about what I'm thinking about while not letting others tell me how to feel or what to think, while I choose to let some questions be unanswered this side of Heaven. Some mysteries are meant to be uncovered in this life here, and there are mysteries that will only be explained in Heaven. We get to be patient as we watch for the mysteries that God reveals for us here. Because the mysteries involve waiting and patience, I am determined to hold the details of life loosely.

Loving people well has little to do with understanding. We don't have to understand in order to love well.

Our minds are wired to understand and search out a thing—or meaning—until we can explain it, repeat it (if it's a good thing), prevent it (if it's not a good thing), and understand, so we can control the outcome next time. Reasons exist for many, many things under the sun, and humans often find comfort in the reasons for something that has happened, but we don't always get the control we desire through natural understanding, though.

Finding the Gold

The word Vilomah is a Sanskrit word that translates into "against the natural order "and is a word used for bereaved parents, similar to how widow or widower are used.

Precious one, are you a Vilomah, too? Healing rides on the wings of forgiveness. Malachi 4:2 (NLT) says, "But for you who fear my name, the Sun of Righteousness will rise with healing in his wings," and I believe this healing comes when we choose forgiveness. Has forgiveness been highlighting itself to you? Maybe again? What could healing and forgiveness produce in your own life? In your thought life? What are you quick to reach for? Is it really helping? What need do you have that is waiting to be truly attended to? Who is your tribe?

FOURTEEN

If Jesus Were Sipping Coffee At My Sink

WOULD JESUS SAY THAT TO ME?

Just because something is globally true does not mean the truth someone else is delivering pertains to the moment I find myself in.
~ Anonymous

The title of this chapter and the significance of this truth came in the nick of time as I was nearing the frayed end of my rope. The anonymous quote is actually my own.

If you are like me, you have repeatedly found yourself in a stinky, soggy bog of poorly chosen words carelessly slung at you by a well-meaning yet terrified Dearheart. People we enjoy, or at a minimum, people we love, have attempted to understand the unimaginable. Sometimes, we try to fill the pause and address tangible pain with words, with something we hope will be helpful or profound instead of embracing silence together. Maybe we try to excuse ourselves from engaging in a more present and perhaps painful shared experience by talking instead of listening. I am not a highly offendable person. Thank God! What that means is I am still able to be offended. Practically speaking, this played out a couple weeks ago when I heard the statement, "God just needed him more in Heaven." I know with every fiber of my being, this is thoroughly untrue. So, I didn't accept it as truth. At that moment, I refused to take offense by simply saying in my heart, "No, thank you." While I tend to lean toward believing the best of people, ever anticipating the gold that's bound to be there, I've still been utterly shocked by the statements made to me about what I hold sacred.

In those moments when our guards are down because we are focusing on something at work or simply minding our own business, these statements can feel like an attack.

The following are actual statements people have said to me. I'm sharing them in hopes that you recognize you aren't alone if someone has said things that aren't helpful or accurate to you. Having been on the receiving end of these (I'm convinced) well-intended statements, I have determined to simply be present with the brokenhearted. Offering a listening heart, silent hugs, and shared tears are powerfully healing.

A family member once said, "Just be happy! He would want you to be happy!"

My response was, "Absolutely, and I completely agree. And he does make me happy. Being apart is hard, though, and I miss him."

Several loved ones have wanted to provide comfort with the well-intended phrase, "He's in a better place."

Also spot on, yet short-sighted, as our grieving is about us and how we experience our loss and separation from him.

We were happy for him! AND simultaneously, we were reeling from the abruptness of his death, the end of our lives as a family unit, and the hopes and dreams we shared with and for Gian. Initially, I just nodded and fought the urge to throw up as I wondered if I heard the statement right. I felt almost, but not quite proud of myself for the graciousness of the response that came out of me quite naturally. Holy Spirit has definitely stepped in to assist me so I can give gentle responses like, "While I am really glad that Gian doesn't have to deal with the issues on the planet like we are, we still want to be with him. Humans were never designed to be separated through death."

My dear friend Amy, a fellow momma in this journey, shared a hurtful inquiry that came from her family member: "You're still sad about that?". . . (That?)

Without hesitation, "Uuuuhhhmmm...yes. I'll probably feel sadness in varying degrees and for many reasons for the rest of my life."

Upon hearing phrases like, "Everything happens for a reason," "If you had stronger faith, the crash wouldn't have happened," and/or "It's all part of God's plan." I have chosen to counter these statements in my own thought life and prayer life versus hashing out the error in public. In my determination to not hurt anyone in my hurting or in being hurt by innocent comments, my smiling silence is the best response.

And ***no***, God is not a vending machine, and we don't get to pick and choose outcomes by saying the right prayers or checking off boxes to guarantee an untouched life. We don't get to play God. While I don't believe arrogance is embedded in the hearts of the people who have uttered these statements, hearing these words out loud is hard, and I can feel as though there is an air of that.

James 1:2-8 for example, tells us not to be dismayed when we experience trials; none of us has promised tomorrow.[i] My faith in God's ability to protect my children remains intact. We were born for eternity, and no amount of hellish accusations will shift my focus from that. Life and death are altogether different than I understood. So much different than I had imagined.

Actually, this is part of God's plan for us...that we are fully convinced of His massive love for us and that we have peace that is bigger[ii] than anything we face. He has done everything for us to be able to prosper on a soulish level in every single way, at every moment, and be in complete health, as all important parts of us prosper, too. He has provided all the help we need--ever. We aren't designed to do these things on our own. Jesus came to give us a hope and a future[iii] and to show Himself faithful to us. He is working all of this for our good and for His glory. Jesus is *not* in the business of killing faithful young men, or our hope, or our dreams.

And when my soul wasn't prospering, not in the least, He remained faithful, kind, patient, and merciful toward me.

One person even told me, "You're like Job. What you have feared has come upon you." As I said earlier, I am not generally offendable. However, This last statement felt like a knife shoved clear through my heart. Accusations like this one have enough poison in them to destroy a person's life.

For anyone trying to make sense of mysteries like ours, it is normal, and Job is an Old Testament man who got robbed. His crumby *friends* tried to make him responsible for what the devil did to him. I'm sure they did this to make themselves feel better and maybe to feel safer. Ultimately, Job received double for all he lost.[iv] Twice the sons and twice the daughters were born to him, twice the blessings in every area of his life, but Job isn't the author of my faith,[v] **Jesus is**. He is stronger than any puny fear I may or may not have had. I am anticipating double for all that's been stolen from me. And the devil will regret ever messing with my family.

"Well, God is in control." This statement is yet another lie commonly believed, sang about and said over and over to Gian's loved ones and me.

Because God is love and love is a free gift, unconditional and without requirements, He, God, chose not to be in control. He chose to be in charge, as evidenced by our free will. He loves us so much that He wants us to choose for ourselves. Just like when my kids were toddlers, and I imagine you know exactly what I mean, as the parents, we were in charge of everything that happened in our home. However, the peanut butter handprint on the window is proof that we were not in control.

People have said some crazy things... I've said some crazy things.

Acknowledging another person's pain and/or suffering is brave and one of the more selfless gifts we can offer. Fear is also a normal reaction to observing the sudden loss experienced by a friend or community member. It's horrifying to realize our families and communities are not exempt from tragedy...but fear doesn't have the power to protect us. It actually interferes with seeing it all clearly and engaging in a healing way. Acknowledging what's happened and the pain, shock, loss, devastation, and injustice simply provides a balm to ease the sting a bit. Studies show that acknowledging a person's pain is what helps to bring comfort, hope, and a willingness to keep trying, and ultimately, this kindness can aid in healing.[vi,vii,viii] Trying to talk someone out of their pain doesn't work. Pain is there for a reason.

When hearing or reading something that grates across my nerves, I ask myself, "If Jesus were here chatting with me in the kitchen, maybe sipping His coffee at my sink, would He say that to me?" Generally, the answer is no. One day, a co-worker I don't care to see again said, "Eventually, you're gonna have to get over it."

"Get over what exactly?" was my response.

This quote says more about the condition of this person's heart and their need for me to make them comfortable with death, which isn't my responsibility. I'm simply not that powerful. (Incidentally, he made that statement while we were in the workplace, completely out of the blue. However, he had no children of his own, and I don't care to defend my love for Gian to those who have no interest in my heart's condition or in understanding how unconditional love works. That's God's job, not mine, and when I finally paused with the Lord and brought that moment to Him, He replied, "You have loved well." That's all He's offered in response.

Sure enough, there's been gold even in the hard, painful half-truths people have said. The gold doesn't just turn up after misspoken words—I've had to go after it. Hearing, "You have loved well," has reinforced my footing and focus, and has helped me let go of offense.

I want to be the person Jesus would invite to stand at His precious friend's sink for that important chat. I want to be trustworthy and safe so that anyone can brave a kitchen sink conversation about the most sacred details of their lives. What a dream to be so trusted. Life-changing conversations happen in those regular moments, like while sipping coffee, and I want to be so heavenly-minded that the nonsense and hurtful things of the world fall away just by being present.

If unconditional love showed up to meet you, like as a person with hair the color of whatever unconditional love's hair would be, and with eyes the shade of unconditional love, with the height, stature, warmth, voice, smile, embrace of unconditional love FOR YOU, designed specifically to get your attention and speak specifically to your heart just the way a really good, safe friend does... you'd recognize *Unconditional Love*, and you'd settle into that meeting. Unconditional Love highlights what needs to be seen. Things like our importance and our significance in the world, that we are loved, whether we've eaten the whole chocolate cake or only half. Unconditional love works hard to show us the way to wholeness while we are missing key parts of ourselves. It's the miraculous substance of Heaven that fills those broken, empty, and missing pieces. Unconditional love supports our hearts as they expand to hold who or what we've lost. Unconditional love also has the hope to embrace who and what is being added to us so that BEAUTY, restoration, redemption, goodness, justice, and God's Glory can be seen all over our story.

That which is God-breathed is glorious, even if it doesn't make sense to us at the time or feels utterly impossible. Just as the worlds were created by what He said in the beginning, our world changes as we accept what He is saying **now**.

Finding the Gold

Truth produces freedom—always. What truth have you hung onto that has led you to freedom? What truth have you been subject to that leads to something else? The most important confrontations occur silently to the outside world while playing out loudly within our own hearts. How are you confronting the words and actions that don't issue peace to your experience?

FIFTEEN

"It's All Gonna Be Okay."

...LIKE HONEY TO MY DRY TOAST...

All that lives forever is love.
~ Steffany Gretzinger

"It's All Gonna Be OK." If that statement had come from anyone else or at any other time, it would have been out of season and certainly not Holy Spirit-inspired. It would have been received as one more fiery dart into my already severely ravaged heart. As I just shared, just because someone *means well* doesn't mean what is delivered is received well. I don't mean that the fear of saying the wrong thing should be the filter we use when wanting to use words in an attempt to comfort or that all words should stop. Not at all! I just want to express that words are powerful and even more impacting than I ever understood until Gian went Home.

When something is Heavenly inspired, though, literally God-breathed, it produces life, peace, hope, joy, confidence, comfort, strength, and healing, ultimately drawing us closer to the God of all creation as our very good Father. Good fathers are safe to be around. They are trustworthy providers, often oozing warmth and wisdom for the questions and situations of life. In my personal experience, the wisdom of my own natural Father frequently looks like a gentle smile, a hug, and silence. There's Heavenly wisdom in that response, too. At times, silence and presence can be the wisest, most generous gift we can give to the hearts around us.

I'm a word person. Words are very important to me and have the ability to really impact me. For instance, there have been words spoken or written to me that have washed over my heart that soothed and calmed the raging inferno inside...much like honey to my dry toast.

For that reason, I have become increasingly selective over the years about the words I choose to both write and speak. Words spoken and written to my family and Gian's loved ones have brought such comfort and nourishment, much like that healthy smear of honey. The honey changes everything! As I shared in the previous chapter, there have been words directed at us that added to our hurt—because of our rawness. Some messages felt like accusations of failure or judgment due to our current grappling with those same lies. The challenging words spoken about mine and Gian's Heavenly Father that insinuate that He chose, allowed, or simply failed to either spare G from the crash or heal him of his injuries are lies. What we need are risky words that come right from the Father's heart for us.

Words and language are such a gift, yet they aren't always the best delivery system to convey what's happening in our hearts. I understand that when people are enduring the unimaginable, enduring heartsmash, we can try to fix what we perceive as broken or damaged or attempt to offer a tidy "solution" with a sweet and well-intended phrase. It is as if saying the right thing is all it takes to remove heartsmash pain from the equation.

The space around us, undoubtedly, during the first five years was uncomfortable and could have been interpreted by people who loved us as void of healthy emotions and thoughts that needed to be corrected with a spiritual Band-Aid. However, more noise only made us feel misinterpreted, tired, alienated, and angry.

My family and I immediately became targets for all kinds of words following the crash and from each end of the word spectrum. Many of them were full of love, kindness, support, and scripture. The most powerfully helpful words were and still are the stories of Gian's life and his impact on his loved ones and those who love him. Sometimes, we don't know how important a person is to us until they are removed from us. We received and still receive all of those words as pure GOLD. Some of my favorite word gifts have come in the form of dreams, visions, and Heavenly encounters where G's loved ones experience Gian showing up, alive and well! Gian's legacy resides in all of those life-filled words and encounters!

I love the Bible and am spending significant time in it again. It is a wellspring of life, and all of it is God-breathed.[i] Not every portion of scripture, however, is to be applied to every situation. A haphazardly applied biblical scripture can inflict harm instead of providing the intended healing and comfort.

God assures us that He is near the brokenhearted, and precious in His sight is the death of His saints.[ii] He comforts all who mourn[iii]...and justice[iv] is His idea.

And He is giving me beauty for my ashes.[v]

"It's all gonna be OK," entered my life just seven months following the crash, as a dear (and very brave) friend offered to go on a trip with me out of state for the weekend. Shannon was one that got closer to us as things got uglier. Anyway, I jumped at the opportunity to get away from home—from that intersection—and to safely be in gatherings where no one knew me, my story, or what I was enduring. I could not stomach any more casual words based on speculation, and I needed to be where it was OK for me not to be OK simply because only my trusted friend knew me. I was DESPERATE to hear from my very good God in regard to the circumstances we were facing each day as we continued to wake up to our new life. It was all thoroughly exhausting, and the legal aspect only added a horrid knowledge of a part of society I had been oblivious to most of my life. I never imagined our son's value as a human being and as a completely innocent victim would ever have to be represented and defended. I felt as if the significance of his life was subject to interpretation, and I wasn't confident in my ability to convey his value in words.

At the time of our weekend away, we were just months away from the first court date, and it felt that with every day, a new development, a new excuse, a different legal angle was presented, and my soul was growing more and more weary as the value of Gian's life seemed to shrink with every legal counter. My every breath was a plea for Heaven's intervention. Honestly, I wanted to be rescued from the torture I was enduring. I was so afraid as I anticipated the upcoming legal proceedings. My mind would swirl each time I tried to fathom how on earth I could ever put words to the magnitude of the impact Gian's eighteen years of life had on his family and on me. My stomach turned with the realization the Judge may not *see* his value and, therefore, not apply the law as fully to the woman responsible for so many years of recorded behavior that ultimately matched the events of that night costing Gian his life. I understood that the outcome of the legal actions would impact our girls and Dadio in ways that I wasn't convinced we'd survive if not weighed accurately.

Thankfully, no sooner had my friend and I arrived at our destination that a purely Heavenly breathed theme began to present itself.

Deep, deep peace awaited our arrival as we pulled into town. Our first stop was a beautiful prayer house. As I had experienced there before, words weren't really necessary as I sat in the Lord's presence. This particular day, all I could think to pray was, "Take me to Heaven. Just take me to Heaven," and as I sat facing out one of the windows, with eyes closed,

> *I watched in my mind's eye as family members and friends came up to Gian with huge, warm smiles and eager bear hug embraces. That moment reminded me of a wedding reception as I watched*

Gian's loved ones come with exuberant joy to embrace him and each other. The celebration and the perfect, complete unity were tangible as I watched! Even the long hair of our female loved ones seemed to be alive and flowing with life and vibrancy in this Heavenly moment.

As soon as the vision started, it was over. Somehow, I understood that the moment I had just witnessed was in the future while still being current, and the significance of it was to help sustain me. In that golden moment, everything felt right and perfect. Absolutely nothing was missing.

That entire July weekend was full of traveling mercies, rest, the kindness of strangers, and words of encouragement. My friend and I sat somewhere in the middle of the sea of chairs, and as worship ended that Sunday, prayer naturally began as the pastor gave a prompt to the people gathered that morning. He said something like, "Church, do what you do best..." I don't remember the specifics of the invitation for prayer that morning, but I raised my hand for those around me to stretch out their kindness and their faith to pray for what God knew I needed. I remember the man next to me. He and his young children paused to pray for me, and then he stopped with tears in his eyes. He just stopped and looked at me and very soberly said, "It's all gonna be OK." As if he knew. While he may not have known the specifics of my life, our life, he definitely *knew* what I needed to hear from our Father. That man's kindness and care were thick and I felt badly, as I recognized aspects of my suffering had invaded that man's understanding as he looked at me with awareness.

To clarify, the Holy Spirit can and does provide knowledge to people who rely on Him to be able to pray for Heaven's resources to enter and impact a given situation. This man felt the compassion of the Lord when he looked at me and was impacted by praying for me, but not negatively. He was able to pray effectively because his own understanding was informed by the Holy Spirit's perfect wisdom of what I needed at that moment. It was so much like an earlier visit of mine where, in the middle of worship, I turned around and blurted out, "You're beautiful!" to a young man sitting behind me. He burst into tears and shared that he had just asked God if it was OK for him to want to be beautiful! Clearly, God thinks it's OK for boys and men to be beautiful!... I've known it for a long time.

> *What a beautiful sight to behold—the precious feet of the messenger coming over the mountains to announce good news!*
>
> —Isaiah 52:7 *TPT*

After the service, an invitation to receive more prayer was released, and I chose to go to the front of the church to receive specific prayer for what I *thought* I needed. Several beautiful and well-trained prayer warriors were lined up along the front of the building, ready to pray with any of us needing Heaven's invasion. As I went forward, a gorgeous young man caught my gaze and smiled at me, motioning for me to come over. With so many people converging in that same area for prayer, too, I had to lean in close to hear him speak and to be heard. I stepped close to my new prayer partner to state my need. His kind eyes locked with mine. As I said the words no momma should ever be in a place to say out loud, this powerful, love-soaked young man wrapped his arms around me and sang over me and my situation, "It's all gonna be OK. It's all gonna be OK." Although that young man looked nothing like my son and sounded nothing like my son, his confidence in the goodness of the God of the universe felt so much like Gian's.

As Jesus' mother did, I tucked all of these treasures in my heart for safe keeping, for ongoing close examination, and for future reference, just as I have since the day Gian was born.

The same dear friend who was on this trip with me has encouraged me to expound on the significance of the phrase, "It's all gonna be OK."

Let me break down each word for you:

Merriam-Webster defines the word "It" as: "used to refer to an explicit or implicit state of affairs or circumstances, a crucial or climactic point."[vi]

The same dictionary defines "is"[vii] as the present tense of BE.

It and is, or it's: referred immediately to the outcome of the legal details, the impact the sentencing would have on us, as no legal action could restore our son to us, and how the sentencing would impact the responsible driver. *It's* goes on to include the condition of our hearts, our lives without the presence of Gian, our hopes and dreams, and the damage done to our trust in humanity. *It's* touched on every mental, emotional, relational, spiritual, and physical struggle and pain as we learned to care for ourselves and each other while experiencing the wild impact of trauma, grief, and seething anger. Every aspect of our being has been impacted. Our hurting was massive and on a cellular level for a very long time.

It's points to all of the unanswerable questions that we both crave answers to and are afraid to have. *It's* is the daily experience of life apart from one of our most important people. The daily ache for his presence and voice, for all that he has been to us, and all that he would have been to each of us personally. We want to experience the joy that G is living, and it's also the desire to share Gian's story in a transparent yet redemptive way to support the continuation of the legacy he was busy creating. I want to help him do the important thing he wants to do. *It's **this*** story, the huge bull's-eye target on our lives that is waiting for the goodness of God to land hard on the areas of our hearts, minds, and lives that will only be satisfied with Heaven itself. Layered in the rings on that target is the splendor of Gian's short, rich life, just waiting for Heaven's timing to bring about the impact of his legacy. Heaven comes to all of it.

All is defined as: "the whole amount, quantity, or extent of... every member or individual component of...the whole number of sum of...EVERY...everybody and everything...TOTALITY."[viii]

All is ALL. Every fine and clunky detail seen and unseen is included and fully attended to. Nothing is left out or neglected.

Gonna describes a future action, represented by the words *going* and *to*. The word "going" is further expressed by the synonyms: advance, procession, progress, prevailing, and approaching. I love prevailing.[ix]

Be interestingly, the intransitive verb of be = "is."[x] Be is defined as: to have an objective existence: have reality or actuality...to have, maintain, or occupy a place, situation, or position...as a prefix (I know, this is a completely different way to look at this word), Be: to a great or greater degree: thoroughly. Bedeck, for instance, is to clothe with finery. The greater degree feels right to me.

OK is defined as "ALL RIGHT." Also, approved, endorse, authorize.[xi]

= It's all gonna be ALL RIGHT. The entirety of that bull's-eye target (every single big and little issue/detail of life) on our chest is prevailing to thorough rightness. Until all is right. I am resting heavily on *it's all gonna be OK* because God said it will be.

It is OK not to be OK yet.

There are times when the death, destruction, loss, robberies, and injustices of life just knock us off our feet and the air completely out of our lungs. God knows this is a day-by-day journey for me, and the want to be OK is all that's needed. God also knows we just can't suddenly make ourselves or our lives OK when we're dealing with more than a bad attitude after a botched coffee bar order, but real and tangible justice.

My Facebook post from August 9, 2018

> *"...on our fireplace mantle. The trouble in having left, or more accurately, having been violently thrown from our "comfort zone," in addition to the stress of the newness of it all, is there are days I recognize the wind has left my sails, and I sit, drifting in the blazing sun. Thirsty, tired, slow, distracted, tearful, irritable. Ironically, the last three days have felt like a stagnant oven to my soul. Yet, every hint of breeze stirs my hope that relief is coming, that my sails will fill again, and that we'll be carried along once more. I'm thankful for hope. Rather than dropping anchor to settle in the heat, I'm cradling it. Imagining my hope, my Anchor riding along on my right hip so much like my toddlers did. Holding my soul's ultimate freedom, my Anchor, in order for freedom, for the winds to pick up and move us, refresh us, show us new things, pique our curiosity, stir our childlikeness. I'm so ready for a cool breeze. I'm ready for my sails to fill again, ready for a kiss from Heaven, a G-bomb, for gold."*

I'll only drop my anchor in HOPE. I'll not allow it to be set anywhere else.

This post mentions the picture I shared of a placard a friend had given us that we placed on our fireplace mantle. The statement on the gift had something to do with comfort zones and leaving them. Have we ever left the port of our comfort zone! We needed to. I'm sure we lost the placard in our last move.

Although I had zero vision of being OK, or for *it* to be OK, or to ever experience anything beyond survival ever again (which was terrifying), I was willing for someone else to have that hope for me. For a time, other people's hope carried me, carried us, and slowly and gently, we began to see that thriving was possible, not in a speedy way, but more like at a laborious snail's pace. Slowly, we began to see that thriving can occur, and it is happening in us, for us. Wholeness is real even while we are not whole in the same way on earth.

Heaven is sustaining us. There is a grace for those of us who want to continue after the unimaginable happens. This grace enables us, strengthens us, holds us together, shelters us, leads us to keep breathing, and enriches us. I love that this grace is part of Heaven's substance for us here. I love that Gian lives where this sustaining, empowering force flows from, and I wonder if he sees this grace operating in our lives. Does grace sparkle? What color is grace? Is grace golden? For those with eyes that see, does grace look heavily clumped over my heart and mind?

Just as the strangeness of the phrase, "It's all gonna be OK," settled as a bedrock for my heart, I pray the same peace that passes all understanding would also settle in your heart. While our minds have the responsibility to navigate schedules, finances, recipes, and the future, our hearts can be firmly seated in Heaven's provisions. Peace, ease, joy, and trust can be ours regardless of what is happening or what has happened as a response to the impossibilities of life on the planet.

My prayer for us,

Bedeck us, God, with Your version of goodness in the land of the living. Bring Heaven to the it we are facing and flood our lives with Your solution to the insurmountable hurts we've encountered. Father, we invite Your grace to meet the broken places; the losses we've endured are too much for us to manage on our own. Heaven come like honey and smear the dry toast of our lives.

G'S JOURNAL ENTRY

GIAN'S OWN WORDS ARE AS FOLLOWS: SPEAK TO OUR present condition with such stunning certainty and beautiful wisdom.

> *A phrase I really like is "It's OK." Those two words have very many possibilities. It's OK to hurt. It's OK to be tired. It's OK to not want to. It's OK to doubt. It's OK to be hungry. It's OK to be cold. It's OK to fail.*
>
> *As an American, how often do we hear the phrase "It's OK" connected to a negative? Think about it. Most Americans have an easy time fixing problems instead of accepting them.*
>
> *However, there is a very important bit. After I say, "It's OK, this is hard," or "It's OK, I can't breathe," I say, "Now, keep going."*
>
> *Even though I walk through the valley of the shadow of death, I will fear no evil, for You are with me. Your rod and your staff they comfort me. Psalm 23:4*
>
> *Life is scary. It doesn't matter how you live it or what you do; there are gonna be things you don't want to do, but you have to do them anyway.*
>
> *William Shakespeare said, "Some are born great, some achieve greatness, and others have greatness thrust upon them." I wonder who I am? I guess it doesn't really matter so long as I become great.*

Yes, sweet boy. You are greater than you have ever known.

Finding the Gold

I hope you really are OK in every way imaginable. However, the longer I am on the planet, I am increasingly aware that most of us are not OK, at least not in every way. What does OK in everything, in all the ways look like for you? Are you willing for Heaven's version of righting to flood your life? What words could you use to invite all the OKs into what is not yet?

....

....

....

....

....

....

....

....

....

....

....

....

....

....

....

....

....

....

....

....

....

....

SIXTEEN

Notes From Year 8

...IS IT ALL OK?

Sometimes you will never
know the value of a moment,
until it becomes a memory.
~ Dr. Seuss

The richness of Dr. Seuss's statement haunts me. Every time my phone rings, I fight anxious feelings and thoughts that one of my loves will move from my present to my memory next. My phone rarely rang until 2015. Yet when I think of phone calls, I go right to the call from Lan and how he told Jeff and me to come immediately—that there had been a crash. He said not to wait, to come now. I hate that Lan had to make that call. He loves Gian, too. Since that Friday, since that phone call, since that Saturday with Gian soaked in hope, and the Sunday he was set free from the tubes, wires, and machines, I'm forever changed. Gian's freedom is so beautiful, and because of the day we came home without him, we honor our hearts and his life by recognizing these precious days. Honestly, I have found that I begin to unravel if I don't create space to connect with my heart. Over-busyness and even the average business of life can create a buffering or disconnect between me and my heart. Eventually, the buffer will give way if I do not pay attention to my own cues. I become edgy, tired, headachy, nauseated, distracted, and sad, and my hope begins to sag.

While even the most thoughtful and well-planned events to recognize Gian are never quite right, ignoring these days would be impossible. We have traveled to other parts of the world in honor of these days and stayed home for other years. We've prepared Gian's favorite meals to share with family, given to charities, participated in food bank drives, hiked, competed in races, participated in 5k races, and stayed for long hours sitting on the floor with the otters in the Otter room at *Debby Dolittle's Petting Zoo.* Last November 6th, we went to an *Arizona Seahawks football game with* new friends and those who know us well. Regardless, wrapping our arms around each other and pausing to acknowledge Gian is all that really matters.

> Whenever the pain feels much too much, I try to remember how much LESS BEAUTIFUL my life would be without ever knowing our kind of love.
>
> — *A BED FOR MY HEART, ANGELA MILLER*

GIAN'S CARHARTT JACKET IS CURRENTLY DRAPED OVER the chair across from me, just like it used to be when we lived in the same home. It feels right to have his things here with our things as they had been. Yet, he's now twenty-six years old in earth years, and I know he'd be living on his own. Sometimes, I imagine he's just stopped by on his way home after work, and that's why his jacket is here again. It's not hard to remember how his jacket fit, where the cuffs rested just above his thumb knuckles. There are small drips of white paint and a little smudge of grease where his left hand would come to wipe across his belly. These signs of life are treasures to us now, and I wish I had asked him to tell me the stories behind his evidence of living an engaged life. Gian's Dadio, his sisters, and I paused, smiling over the smudges and paint drips to imagine how they got there. We've wondered what adventure he'd been on with his friends. Maybe the grease is from tinkering on the motorcycle he didn't tell us he bought. That's a real thing and an additional bike to the one he helped load into his co-worker's truck that Friday. This second motorcycle was carefully kept at Lan's home for years following the crash. We just didn't know *how* we could remove something so personal from Gian's loved ones. Eventually, my dad and Jeff brought the bike to our home, and then eventually, it was parked in my parent's garage next to my dad's Harley for a long time. I wonder if the jacket would even fit the full-grown man version of him or if he'd still have the bike. Maybe he would have gifted both to his sisters or traded the bike for something bigger and faster.

It's not wrong to miss the person, the people we love, the life we loved, the opportunities we were excited about then, and the community we cared about. Missing Gian is a very real part of my loving him. It's a normal part of my life as I don't just love him; I like him. I enjoyed being with him. I imagine I will always remember him and miss him in the same breaths.

Eight years in, and I can tell you with all certainty that our love hasn't faded, changed, or lessened. These eight years have further driven me to fierceness in opposing the death of the world's children and of our dreams for their future. I simply cannot allow the devil to keep stealing unattested.

What used to be a jarring shock is now more normalized as we are much more functional than we were five years ago and strikingly more so than initially. We are more acclimated to life without his physical presence and to what happened. I have no problem spitting my toothpaste out now. (That's probably good news for anyone wondering.)We are typically sleeping, eating, laughing, learning, reading, trusting, loving, hugging, planning, crying, adventuring, and dreaming much more readily and more peacefully. We are significantly more at ease with what has not changed. This is proof that miracles do happen.

However, being acclimated is not the same as allowing the rock to stay in my shoe. I am now quite familiar with how it feels when a new layer of grief is triggered by offense, anger, sadness, disappointment, regret, blame, death, or injustice is exposed by something I encounter in life. Each is justified, but none of it is meant to stay unaddressed or be carried indefinitely without processing. The little rocks can sneak in and eventually cause bigger problems if we don't stop what we're doing to get them out.

As I drove around doing errands yesterday, the shooting pain that had radiated so frequently through my chest, shoulders, esophagus, and teeth happened again for the first time in a long while. As I paused in that pain, I reverted to, "Jesus, please help." The shooting pain quickly subsided this time, and I gratefully recognized that trauma no longer has the grip on me it used to.

> ...and she loved a boy very, very much-- even more than she loved herself.
>
> — *THE GIVING TREE, SHEL SILVERSTEIN*

We are recognizing the beauty of life in us and around us. The gold of Gian's life and the gold associated with the goodness of God is easier to see and continues to be seen in tangible ways. Maybe it's that we now readily recognize what's been here, what's been happening all along, and yet we still struggle. We still gasp for air sometimes, and I still cry myself to sleep sometimes. Love is like that. Gian is still my first true love. The exposed gold, combined with time, has only solidified that reality. As my friend Amy says, "We are one day closer." Each day, we are one day closer to being together again.

I see hearts everywhere now. Gian gave me my first heart-shaped rock when he was maybe three years old. I still have it, and it's currently resting on top of a sun-bleached, smooth but scarred, palm-sized, heart-shaped coral, which was gifted to me by my brother-in-love. This piece of coral has two deep scars and a puncture.

Just four months after the crash in March of 2016, several family members decided a dramatic change in scenery was imperative to all of our survival. They weren't wrong! We definitely needed *something*. Dadio and the girls had been to Maui two years before and were eager to return. They believed the sun, sand, and intensity of the beauty would be healing for all of us.

The heart-shaped coral was discovered while we were walking on one of the beaches. My brother-in-love said it must be for me as it looked just like my heart. I understood then that removing anything from the beaches is forbidden. No sand, no rocks, and no coral are allowed to be removed from the Hawaiian Islands to, very importantly, preserve the islands themselves. Additionally, there is a legend that extreme bad luck will follow anyone who does. Someone told us that the post offices receive hundreds of packages each year with sand, rocks, and coral in them after bad luck had fallen on some of these treasure keepers. While I didn't necessarily believe in the warning of the legend, I had zero desire to take something that didn't belong to me. So, the heart-shaped coral stayed in the condo for a few days as I admired it. As we neared our time to leave, I struggled with the idea of leaving the coral behind, so I asked a local for advice.

Later that day, I found a young man working further down the beach, and so I posed my dilemma. He replied, "You are a kind and loving woman. Ask the island, and she will tell you." I was shocked and grateful for his gracious direction, and so I did. Having carved out a few minutes by myself, I waded into the waves and asked Maui if I could keep the beautiful treasure she had lovingly encouraged me with. It was as if Maui answered with a warm hug and a very generous "yes." This first yes would be just the beginning of so many more kisses from Heaven showing up as hearts in very regular details.

And a lot has happened in the last eight years. We sold our family home to eliminate the terror of empty spaces, bought a condo (way downsized, and I totally recommend it), and moved across town away from that intersection. We changed jobs, and Dadio bought and built out a van for adventuring. The girls graduated from High School and have both moved out. One daughter has made us grandparents to cats and chickens and given us a grandson through marriage.

Belle chose to represent her brother with a single red rose during her vow exchange on a beach in Spain. Before leaving the beach, she and her sweetheart walked into the waves so her hubby could throw Gian's rose as far out into the surf as he could. As they made their way back up the beach, Belle turned to see the rose had ridden the waves up onto the sand and away from the surf. Another couple walking by saw the rose, picked it up, and took it with them. May the goodness of Gian's life bless them in profound ways, too.

I've only recently learned that our son-in-love gives G's ashes a fist bump every morning as he passes by. It's also curious to me that his handwriting looks so much like Gian's.

The younger of our daughters refers to us as Nana and Grampa for her puppy.

Her sweetheart was hand-picked by longtime friends of hers. This darling young couple explained that Gian would really like him, and I could easily see why. It's easy to believe that's true for so many reasons. This sweetheart and the young man who "picked" him for Zosia also work in the same pipe fitting shop that G so enjoyed.

We've explored other countries, and sure enough, our hearts were there, too. Running away from our life may work for forty-eight hours, but that's the max I've discovered for any kind of escape attempt to last. My heart always finds me, always finds us. Time zones do have a lot of influence, but they don't affect things like that. Jeff has climbed mountains and bombed down them, too. Early on, he considered diving off of one mountain in particular. I'm glad he's chosen otherwise, and I understand.

We've now moved out of state to follow our deep need for more sunshine, dry skies, and fresh perspective. We've made new friends while continuing to cherish our fire-forged ones. I still wear a gold G charm on my necklace, as do a few of our family members. Some of us still wear our memorial bracelets. Mine stays on day and night. Several of us have tattoos in honor of him. A few precious girls in Gian's world were gifted rose gold rings that were purchased with his death fund. I wear mine on my right pointer finger. Victims of homicide are eligible for the death fund. I'm not a fan of that, but I made sure those dollars went to lasting good use.

The natural progression of our parenting now includes the opportunity (with a TON of help from friends) to figure out the application, approval, and installation processes for memorial road signs. The requirement for this privilege includes death by vehicular homicide. Meeting that requirement also means we are now a certain kind of fun...not the typical kind of fun we had hoped for, though. We share identical messaging language on our signs (the only two of their kind in the state of Washington) with the House family. Their beautiful eighteen-year-old son also went Home due to a reckless driver (alcohol was in the vehicle) just twelve days after Gian. Within a short time of our boys going Home, we were introduced by a mutual friend and became fast friends. I have fallen head over heels in love with them. I never in my wildest imagination could have dreamt that part of my motherhood would include discovering memorial road sign laws, much less with this incredible family, or that we'd have so many of the fine details in common with local Dearhearts.

And yet, there are so many of *us*. Each life is precious and sacred. Every one of their stories is so different than mine. In addition to the House's K., there's also Lori's Sarah, Marki's Joshua Robert and Josh Cody, Abra's Nathan, Ann's Brandon, Jan's Sean, Sharley's Daunte, Liza's Jackson, Jenny's Jenna, Shiela's Ally, Amy's Keigen, Pauli's Kaitlyn, Renea's Lacy, Tasha's Lucas, Carly's Hunter, Buddy's Carter, Mark's Jack, Misty's Trent and Lou's Eric. Of course, our children don't just belong to us; they also belong to our families and communities. Many in this beautiful company paved the way and let us know that Heaven would be entering our lives like we couldn't have fathomed and that we could keep breathing simply because they were still breathing (and curiously so beautifully breathing) by the time we joined them. Incredible.

Little did I know that I'd also provide evidence and hope to the ones who joined after me that survival is possible. Now I get it. At some point, we all go Home. All of us. Timing and fairness are obviously not within our interpretation or control, and clearly, we aren't granted participation in the *approval* process. While we don't have to endure it, there's no other option. Many of us have additional children to stay present for and have chosen to love each other really well. Catching each other's tears and giving sips of water between sobs is one example of what I mean by loving each other well. I feel so safe with these people.

As horrid as it is to say, I'm incredibly grateful for those I've met ONLY because our children went Home before us. Our paths would've never crossed otherwise. The list is much longer and is full to overflowing with some of the most awe-inspiring humans, and we *get* each other. I'm so grateful for that part, as much as I despise it. I often think to myself, *These are the most beautiful human beings...how did we get lumped together in this horror?!* Being a *good* person wasn't enough to prevent bad things from happening to us and our loved ones. I've wondered if God and our kids knew how grateful we'd be to have each other's company, and so they (because God is good like that) made sure we would get introduced. He knew I'd quickly fall in love with them, their children, their scars, and their hearts. We've agreed that if I come across a magic wand that I will wish them out of our lumped horror. That I will do in a heartbeat. As grateful as I am for each of them, I don't want them here with me. While no one is welcome, I won't turn anyone away, and I am always so grateful when someone says, "I just can't imagine." I don't want anyone else to understand.

And I will always wonder about our Peter Pan kind of brood of youngsters full of joy, ready to adventure, and so carefree now, as the bunch of them are there in Heaven together living their best lives. I imagine our kids have joined together because of us because we've lost them. We have found each other; surely they have found each other too. Maybe it's the other way around. When I close my eyes, I can see them rambling around Heaven, laughing, adventuring, and running with their fists flying, jumping, and spinning, with victorious shouts echoing all around them. I wonder if they all, kind of in a rough and tumbly kind of way, pile into a cozy spot to gaze at the ones they left on Earth. I wonder if they watch us in those big Earthy celebratory moments when we sing "Happy Birthday." Are they singing, too? Are they happily witnessing as wedding vows are exchanged and when babies enter the light? Babies are straight from Heaven. Every level-headed person knows it's true. Puppies are straight from Heaven, too, but babies are especially from Heaven.

Since November 6, 2015 I am less and less concerned about everything, except for hearts. Hearts matter to me, and acknowledging them matters to me. Pausing from my tasks to acknowledge what is going gloriously well for some and the struggles of others has become vital to my own well-being. The endurance that life requires of our hearts is important to shine a spotlight on now and then. Most of us are involved in a marathon of sorts that we didn't necessarily pay the entrance fee for either. There's been a precious few that have stopped to say, "I see you." "I remember." Not that I am waiting for it anymore, but these little encouragements feel like kisses from Heaven.

Is it ALL OK?

Yes.

AND...allowing OK requires work, trust, and honesty. The simplest, most peaceful way for me to approach living is to accept and commit to living one heartbeat, one minute at a time. There's nothing to get anxious about in those micro-moments and when I allow myself to rest right there. I can feel Heaven and Gian close. He lives in the presence of God, and God has promised to be with us always, even to the end of time.[i] He is in the air we breathe. All is OK, actually righted, as my focus is turned Heavenward.

My work is simple; love the one in front of me while allowing the goodness of God to do what the goodness of God does. Also, I ask for eyes to see it, ears to hear it, and a heart to understand and receive the goodness and love of God.[ii] I don't want one drop of His goodness to go unnoticed by me or to be wasted in my life or in the lives of my loved ones. In all honesty, I love practically everyone.

Trusting is an act of my will, and since I'm being transparent, trusting is often a practice of my physical self. Trusting does not look like frantic, spastic rushing to solve *problems*. Trusting often looks like pausing to turn my focus and my affection toward Heaven as I share my heart with our very good God and then listen as He shares His heart and thoughts with me. Trusting looks like waiting for the way forward to be revealed, even if it is only a step or a breath at a time as I follow peace. Ultimately, I am in His hands. My future is secure; my destiny is established. Sometimes, trusting is laughing hard at life.

Honesty is that same heart posture. In my bright, hope-filled moments and in the ones that exude nothing of the sort, I will be completely through and through, honest with God and a precious, saintly, supernatural few because I don't want to hurt anyone with my hurting or my processing. Honesty is a must, though. Our words are so powerful. The wrestle that happens in my mind is less frequent as I've learned to bring the brutal stuff, my questions, and the mysteries of life to God for Him to attend to. Often, I don't use or even have words at all to accurately express what I'm feeling or experiencing, so I just invite Him into what's happening in my heart and mind, and He miraculously infuses those moments with His own heart for me and for what matters to me.

Somehow, I come away knowing I am treasured, cared for, and understood. I feel more peaceful and convinced that the details of my life and heart are treasured by God Himself. Every moment of every day, I am held together by His goodness, kindness, patience, love, and grace. Grace is a powerful force.

It's then that sharing with my loved ones reveals the heart of our very good Father and not the heart of an acid-drenched daughter. Humanity isn't designed with the capacity to endure the things I'd say out loud in those ugly human moments.

I used to think that having limitations on my out-loud honesty was a form of dishonesty, but I understand the difference more completely now. Since our words create worlds, I want to contribute to the hearts around me intentionally by not parroting what the enemy of my soul says but really listening to the heart of the Father and then releasing those words from Him.

Now I understand, I've been whole in my heartsmash, broken open-ness all along the journey. Traumatic loss and the death of a child or of a loved one is devastating. Period. Feeling the enormity of that devastation is healthy and right. *Feeling it needs to happen.* It's a must, really. Suffering doesn't mean we aren't whole; rather, it indicates something big happened. What is exposed can be cared for and healed, and yet healing doesn't restore my heart to its previous state. Instead, healing changed my heart completely. My heart has been expanded in necessary ways, it does not resemble its previous self very much at all. And I'm being healed every day. While I recognize the same *garden* from my time on the living room floor with Jesus, it doesn't function like it did before the crash.

And there's the OK--the all things being well and the *ALL will be righted* promise that is actively being accomplished in our lives. I am experiencing more of the *all being well*, although there seems to be a kind of tidal ebb and flow movement or shifting that occurs. Nothing in this life is truly static. Not even concrete is immune to the forces of nature. As much as it is more and more accurate to say, "Yes, all is OK," it is also accurate to say that OK is being worked out on a moment-to-moment, day-to-day, and layer-by-layer basis as we encounter the natural aspects of life. I have vision-ish for the *it's all gonna be OK* promise. God is in the moment to moment. Right now, is all we have anyway. The ebbs and flows of joy, of seasons, and of laughter help to create richness and miracle moments that contain less fear and less pain. Perfect love *continues* to drive out all fear.[iii]

It's all gonna be OK, is the promise I am experiencing in an increasing manner as *Perfect Love* works through the layers of my heart, my mind, and my life. Each day provides me an opportunity to watch for it. And so I am.

From my Facebook post dated June 3, 2023

"Brother is such a beautiful word." After a rough night, I finally left bed early this morning. As I sat on the floor (it's just what I do) with the Lord, I heard that phrase. He gave us that word, title, and role, after all. Brothers are His idea, as is the significance of their presence.

One of my favorite authors, Tom Zuba, has discussed how the Bereaved become the teachers. I don't love the truth of this reality, and yet I'm grateful for the opportunity to learn and do better.

Grief is an honest, powerful teacher. As are brothers.

From one Momma to another, current or future, to my friends, please consider teaching your "children" to sit with their empathy and their memories AND encourage them to do something with all of that. One of the most stunning heartsmashes I've experienced is to witness my children's ongoing suffering. I can't make it better. Gone are the days that I could kiss an owie to have some measure of relief come to them. This owie can't be kissed away so easily as every day presents a new layer, a new loss, a new loneliness.

Having said that, I've become slightly better at reaching out when someone comes to mind. I've taken the time to write important dates on my calendar and create a little bit of time to follow up with my care and awareness. A small gesture like a personal text or dropping a card in the mail can yield incredible comfort, especially with the passage of time. This was our 8th birthday apart from Gian, and I'm AMAZED that our little family has lasted this long.

A miracle of sorts.

Please DO learn from our experience. No one replaces your love. No one replaces your kindness. No one replaces your presence.

#withGianAlways #heavenlyMindedMomma

~Alanna

Finding the Gold

We are all collecting something or somethings, as we travel through life. What are you collecting? What are you drawn to? Why? Are these somethings golden to you, helpful to you, bringing healing, or encouragment? How?

Afterword

One day, during the COVID-19 pandemic, I chose to go for a walk. I know, GASP. It was a sunny afternoon, and only to the stop sign at the end of the street in my neighborhood. As a nation, we were told to stay home to flatten the curve. The only sounds I heard were the birds chirping and leaves rustling in the breeze. Zero cars on the road. It was really lovely, actually. I desperately needed to get sunshine into my eyes, move my body a bit, and clear my racing thoughts.

I had dedicated myself to learning how to proactively protect my family, friends, neighbors, and the world...while working feverishly to familiarize myself with government requirements.

All of us had a lot on our minds and hearts, and it really showed.

As I walked, I talked to God about it all. Clearly, I was no stranger to death or other scary things, and obviously, God already knew that. So, I began to process the little information, the very little I understood about the virus at that time, about the requirements/limitations, while simultaneously witnessing loved ones be impacted in very, very serious ways. It was all terrifying.

The second I stopped talking about all the COVID stuff (actually, I was pretty much only pausing to take a breath), He said, “Stay out of the weeds. Look up!”

His instruction for me hasn’t changed since then, and He wasn’t telling me to not *know* the weeds are there—only to stay out of them and to **shift my gaze Heavenward**.

I bless you to *look up. Look up to Unconditional Love*, and continue looking up.

Resources of Companionship & Joy

The following resources have provided moments of companionship and encouragement along my journey. I hope these gems meet you in similar ways. I am particularly fond of authors and creators who cheer on my processing, the ones who don't just tell me how to feel or what to think, and in my darkest moments, I needed to know that bad things have happened to other "good" or at least very average people too. Having said that, I am the first to admit that my thinking has also needed to be challenged, so the list goes beyond feel-good reads. When we challenge what we think, what we believe can be the key to our thriving on this side of Heaven and amid extreme challenges.

Full disclosure: More than one of these books has been chucked at my bedroom wall because the author made me angry. I don't know if Jeff remembers or not. Still, I refused to pick a few of them up off the bedroom floor until I had forgiven the author for whatever crazy thing they wrote that I couldn't stomach. The point is not agreement. The point is learning, healing, thinking, and challenging our beliefs. This is part of healing and of really living. For as long as humanity has been on the planet, we've needed each other just as frequently as we've hurt each other. Iron sharpening iron is required for us to survive the threats hiding in our daily lives. Thriving to me was only a notion—a concept—for a long while until the companionship I discovered in the following books and movies encouraged me to keep looking up and to stay engaged.

When I decided to learn about Heaven, it was a pivotal key to increasing my peace and my hope. Ministers like Dean Braxton and Kat Kerr (along with many others) have personal experiential knowledge of Heaven. Visit www.katkerr.com and www.deanbraxton.com for their personal stories and resources. Elijah Stream Ministries at https://elijahstream.com provides healthy, biblically strong insights that have helped me navigate this life.

MOVIES: In addition to watching all light-hearted comedies because laughing is good medicine, please consider these too.

- *Inside Out*
- *Peanut Butter Falcon*
- *Up*
- *Bridge to Terabithia*
- *August Rush*
- *Facing the Giants*
- *Ratatouille*
- *50 First Dates*
- *How to Train Your Dragon*
- *Brother Bear*
- *Princess Bride*
- *Big Fish*
- *Holes*
- *Hook*
- *Flushed Away*
- *Despicable Me*
- *The Blind Side*
- *The Secret Life of Walter Mitty*

BOOKS:

- *Permission to Mourn, A New Way To Do Grief*, by Tom Zuba
- *The Shack*, by William Paul Young
- *Heart Made Whole*, by Christa Black Gifford
- *Tear Soup: A Recipe for Healing After Loss*, by Pat Schweibert, Chuck DeKlyen, and Taylor Bills
- *Loving Our Kids On Purpose*, by Danny Silk
- *Where Was God On The Worst Day Of My Life*, by Jonathan Foster
- *Almost Everything, Notes on Hope*, by Anne Lamott
- *Brush Strokes of Grace*, by Andrew Worley
- *In Heaven! Experiencing The Throne Of God*, by Dean Braxton
- *Forgiving What You Can't Forget*, by Lysa Terkeurst
- *It's Not Supposed To Be This Way: Finding Unexpected Strength When Disappointments Leave You Shattered*, by Lysa Terkeurst
- *Imagine Heaven: Near-Death Experiences*, by John Burke
- *The Boy, the Mole, the Fox and the Horse*, by Charlie Mackesy
- *Into the Light, Real Life Stories about Angelic Visits, Visions of the Afterlife and Other Pre-death Experiences*, by John Lerma, M.D.
- *No More Faking Fine, Ending the Pretending*, by Esther Fleece
- *This Naked Mind: Control Alcohol, Find Freedom, Discover Happiness & Change Your Life (Volume 1)*, by Annie Grace
- *God's Best Friend, the Adventures of an Ordinary Man and an Extraordinary God*, by Gabriel Lopez

- *Daring Greatly, How the Courage to Be Vulnerable Transforms the Way We Live, Love, Parent, and Lead*, by Brené Brown, Ph.D., LMSW
- *The Giving Tree* by Shel Silverstein

If you're like me and have been impacted by an impaired driver, or suspect that is the case, MADD, Mothers Against Drunk Driving, may be a source of support for you. The organization website is https://madd.org.

To locate an EMDR provider, I recommend using this search engine: www.psychologytoday.com.

Author's Note

Beloved Reader, thank you. Thank you for joining me here. So very brave of you. I pray for an increase in your hope, in our hope. That the Creator of all that we see, of the whole earth, and everything we don't see yet, would meet you right where you are, in whatever condition your hope is in. That Jesus, the Man of Sorrows, would comfort, heal, and restore every bit of damaged joy. Thank You, Lord, that all we need to say to is: "Yes. Welcome in. My heart is Yours, Jesus. Help it all, as only You can."

Endnotes

INTRODUCTION

i. "Well-being." In *Merriam-Webster Dictionary*, July 21, 2025. https://www.merriam-webster.com/dictionary/well-being.

1. NOVEMBER 6, 2015

i. Tucker, Chris. "Serious Five-vehicle Crash at Kitsap and National in Bremerton." *Kitsap Daily News*, October 24, 2016. https://www.kitsapdailynews.com/news/serious-five-vehicle-crash-at-kitsap-and-national-in-bremerton/.

2. HOPE, KINDNESS, & GRACE

i. John 10:10 (*New King James Version*): "The thief does not come except to steal, and to kill, and to destroy. I have come that they may have life, and that they may have *it* more abundantly."
ii. Isaiah 61:3 (*New King James Version*): "To console those who mourn in Zion, to give them beauty for ashes, the oil of joy for mourning, the garment of praise for the spirit of heaviness; that they may be called trees of righteousness, the planting of the Lord, that He may be glorified."
iii. Zuba, Tom. "Choose Light." In *Permission to Mourn*. Bish Press, 2014.

3. ANNE'S PRAYER

i. Psalm 126:5 (*New King James Version*): "Those who sow in tears Shall reap in joy."

4. POSTURE OF FORGIVENESS

i. Luke 6:31 (*New King James Version*): "And just as you want men to do to you, you also do to them likewise."
ii. Nehemiah 8:10 (*New King James Version*): "Then he said to them, 'Go your way, eat the fat, drink the sweet, and send portions to those for whom nothing is prepared; for *this* day *is* holy to our Lord. Do not sorrow, for the joy of the LORD is your strength.'"

iii. Exodus 21:23-25 (*New King James Version*): "But if *any* harm follows, then you shall give life for life, eye for eye, tooth for tooth, hand for hand, foot for foot, burn for burn, wound for wound, stripe for stripe."
iv. Psalm 103:12 (*New King James Version*): "As far as the east is from the west, *So* far has He removed our transgressions from us."
v. 1 Corinthians 13:4-7 (*New King James Version*): "Love suffers long *and* is kind; love does not envy; love does not parade itself, is not puffed up; does not behave rudely, does not seek its own, is not provoked, thinks no evil; does not rejoice in iniquity, but rejoices in the truth; bears all things, believes all things, hopes all things, endures all things."
vi. "First Step Toward Forgiveness | Tony Evans," n.d. https://go.tonyevans.org/blog/first-step-toward-forgiveness.

"ZOSIA'S TREASURE"

i. 1 Peter 5:8-10 (*New King James Version*): "Be sober, be vigilant; because your adversary the devil walks about like a roaring lion, seeking whom he may devour. Resist him, steadfast in the faith, knowing that the same sufferings are experienced by your brotherhood in the world. But may the God of all grace, who called us to His eternal glory by Christ Jesus, after you have suffered a while, perfect, establish, strengthen, and settle *you.*"

5. THAT MOMENT IN MY UNZIPPED HEART

i. Proverbs 4:23 (*New Kings James Version*): "Keep your heart with all diligence, For out of it *spring* the issues of life."
ii. Psalm 34:18 (*New King James Version*): "The LORD *is* near to those who have a broken heart, And saves such as have a contrite spirit."
iii. Isaiah 53:3 (*New King James Version*): "He is despised and rejected by men, A Man of sorrows and acquainted with grief. And we hid, as it were, *our* faces from Him; He was despised, and we did not esteem Him."

6. TRANSFORMATIVE LOVE

i. John 15:13 (*New King James Version*): "Greater love has no one than this, than to lay down one's life for his friends."
ii. Etienne de Grellet, quoted in *The Oxford Dictionary of Quotations*, 5th ed. (Oxford: Oxford University Press, 1999), 319. "I shall pass this way but once. Any good that I can do or any kindness I can show to any human being, let me do it now. Let me not defer nor neglect it, for I shall not pass this way again."
iii. "Love the One You're With by Stephen Stills," *Genius*, accessed July 22, 2025 https://genius.com/Stephen-stills-love-the-one-youre-with-lyrics. The song was inspired by Billy Preston's tagline, "If you can't be with the one

you love, love the one you're with," which Stills asked permission to use. The song peaked at #14 on the Billboard Hot 100 in 1970.

iv. Acts 5:15-17 (*New King James Version*): "And believers were increasingly added to the Lord, multitudes of both men and women, so that they brought the sick out into the streets and laid *them* on beds and couches, that at least the shadow of Peter passing by might fall on some of them. Also a multitude gathered from the surrounding cities to Jerusalem, bringing sick people and those who were tormented by unclean spirits, and they were all healed."

v. Hebrews 12:2 (*New King James Version*): "Looking unto Jesus, the author and finisher of *our* faith, who for the joy that was set before Him endured the cross, despising the shame, and has sat down at the right hand of the throne of God."

vi. John 19:30 (*New King James Version*): "So when Jesus had received the sour wine, He said, 'It is finished!" And bowing His head, He gave up His spirit.'"

vii. Martin Luther King Jr., *Letter from Birmingham Jail*, April 16, 1963, in *Why We Can't Wait* (New York: Signet Classics, 2000), 86. "Injustice anywhere is a threat to justice everywhere. We are caught in an inescapable network of mutuality, tied in a single garment of destiny. Whatever affects one directly, affects all indirectly."

7. SO MUCH JOY!

i. Isaiah 61:3 (*King James Version*): "To appoint unto them that mourn in Zion, to give unto them beauty for ashes, the oil of joy for mourning, the garment of praise for the spirit of heaviness; that they might be called trees of righteousness, the planting of the LORD, that he might be glorified."

ii. Psalm 27:13 (*New King James Version*): "I would have lost heart, unless I had believed That I would see the goodness of the LORD In the land of the living."

iii. Hebrews 12:2 (*King James Version*): "Looking unto Jesus, the author and finisher of *our* faith, who for the joy that was set before Him endured the cross, despising the shame, and has sat down at the right hand of the throne of God."

"A RETURN TO CIVILITY"

i. Mark 12:31 (*King James Version*): "And the second is like, namely this, Thou shalt love thy neighbour as thyself. There is none other commandment greater than these."

ii. "Civilité — Definition & Quiz," Ultimate Lexicon, December 21, 2025.

iii. "Civility Noun - Definition, Pictures, Pronunciation and Usage Notes |

Oxford Advanced Learner's Dictionary at OxfordLearnersDictionaries.Com."

iv. "Roman Law and Its Lasting Influence on the Legal System of Europe | Ancient Origins."

v. "The Rules of Civility," by The Mount Vernon Ladies' Association, George Washington's Mount Vernon, accessed January 14, 2026, https://www.mountvernon.org/george-washington/rules-of-civility.

vi. Matthew 7:12 (*King James Version*): "Therefore all things whatsoever ye would that men should do to you, do ye even so to them: for this is the law and the prophets."

9. SECOND CHANCES OR MERCY VERSUS NINETH CHANCE

i. "Accident." In *Merriam-Webster Dictionary*, July 22, 2025. https://www.merriam-webster.com/dictionary/accident.

ii. "Mercy." In *Merriam-Webster Dictionary*, July 26, 2025. https://www.merriam-webster.com/dictionary/mercy.

iii. Lamentations 3:22-24 (*New King James Version*): "Through the Lord's mercies we are not consumed, Because His compassions fail not. They are new every morning; Great is Your faithfulness. 'The Lord is my portion,' says my soul, 'Therefore I hope in Him!'"

11. FINALLY, A DREAM!

i. Judges 6:12 (*New King James Version*): "And the Angel of the LORD appeared to him, and said to him, 'The LORD *is* with you, you mighty man of valor!'"

ii. "Luke 19 NKJV," n.d. https://biblehub.com/nkjv/luke/19.htm.

iii. Matthew 25:23 (*New King James Version*): "His lord said to him, 'Well *done,* good and faithful servant; you have been faithful over a few things, I will make you ruler over many things. Enter into the joy of your lord.'"

13. SURVIVING TO THRIVING

i. Menander. *Time heals all wounds.* Quoted in "Time Heals All Wounds." *Grammarist.* Accessed July 27, 2025. https://grammarist.com/proverb/time-heals-all-wounds/.

ii. Admin. "What Is EMDR? - EMDR Institute - EYE MOVEMENT DESENSITIZATION AND REPROCESSING THERAPY." EMDR Institute - EYE MOVEMENT DESENSITIZATION AND REPROCESSING THERAPY, December 3, 2024. https://www.emdr.com/what-is-emdr/.

iii. Psalm 27:13 (*New King James Version*): "*I would have lost heart,* unless I had believed That I would see the goodness of the LORD In the land of the living."

iv. Luther, Martin. *"You cannot keep birds from flying over your head but you can keep them from building a nest in your hair."* Quoted in Gigault. "'You Cannot Keep Birds From Flying Over Your Head but You Can Keep Them From Building a Nest in Your Hair' - OMI Lacombe." *OMI Lacombe*, March 29, 2023. https://omilacombe.ca/you-cannot-keep-birds-from-flying-over-your-head-but-you-can-keep-them-from-building-a-nest-in-your-hair/.

14. IF JESUS WERE SIPPING COFFEE AT MY SINK

i. James 1:2-8 (*New King James Version*): "My brethren, count it all joy when you fall into various trials, knowing that the testing of your faith produces patience. But let patience have *its* perfect work, that you may be perfect and complete, lacking nothing. If any of you lacks wisdom, let him ask of God, who gives to all liberally and without reproach, and it will be given to him. But let him ask in faith, with no doubting, for he who doubts is like a wave of the sea driven and tossed by the wind. For let not that man suppose that he will receive anything from the Lord; *he is* a double-minded man, unstable in all his ways."

ii. Phillipians 4:7 (*New King James Version*): "And the peace of God, which surpasses all understanding, will guard your hearts and minds through Christ Jesus."

iii. Jeremiah 29:11 (*New King James Version*): "For I know the thoughts that I think toward you, says the LORD, thoughts of peace and not of evil, to give you a future and a hope."

iv. Job 42:10 (*New King James Version*): "And the Lord restored Job's losses when he prayed for his friends. Indeed the Lord gave Job twice as much as he had before."

v. Hebrews 12:2 (*New King James Version*): "Looking unto Jesus, the author and finisher of *our* faith, who for the joy that was set before Him endured the cross, despising the shame, and has sat down at the right hand of the throne of God."

vi. LaChapelle, Diane L, Susan Lavoie, and Ainsley Boudreau. "The Meaning and Process of Pain Acceptance. Perceptions of Women Living With Arthritis and Fibromyalgia." *Pain Research and Management* 13, no. 3 (January 1, 2008): 201–10. https://doi.org/10.1155/2008/258542.

vii. Edlund, Sara M., Maria L. Carlsson, Steven J. Linton, Alan E. Fruzzetti, and Maria Tillfors. "I See You're in Pain – the Effects of Partner Validation on Emotions in People With Chronic Pain." *Scandinavian Journal of Pain* 6, no. 1 (August 13, 2014): 16–21. https://doi.org/10.1016/j.sjpain.2014.07.003.

viii. Linton, S.J., K. Boersma, K. Vangronsveld, and A. Fruzzetti. "Painfully Reassuring? The Effects of Validation on Emotions and Adherence in a Pain Test." *European Journal of Pain* 16, no. 4 (August 31, 2011): 592–99. https://doi.org/10.1016/j.ejpain.2011.07.011.

15. "IT'S ALL GONNA BE OKAY."

i. 2 Timothy 3:16-17 (*New King James Version*): "Scripture *is* given by inspiration of God, and *is* profitable for doctrine, for reproof, for correction, for instruction in righteousness, that the man of God may be complete, thoroughly equipped for every good work."
ii. Psalm 116:15 (*New King James Version*): "Precious in the sight of the LORD *Is* the death of His saints."
iii. Matthew 5:4 (*New King James Version*): "Blessed *are* those who mourn, For they shall be comforted."
iv. Isaiah 1: 17 (*New King James Version*): "Learn to do good; Seek justice, Rebuke the oppressor; Defend the fatherless, Plead for the widow."
v. Isaiah 6:13 (*New King James Version*): "To console those who mourn in Zion, To give them beauty for ashes, The oil of joy for mourning, The garment of praise for the spirit of heaviness; That they may be called trees of righteousness, The planting of the LORD, that He may be glorified."
vi. "It." In *Merriam-Webster Dictionary*, n.d. https://www.merriam-webster.com/dictionary/it.
vii. "Is." In *Merriam-Webster Dictionary*, n.d. https://www.merriam-webster.com/dictionary/is.
viii. "All." In *Merriam-Webster Dictionary*, May 31, 2025. https://www.merriam-webster.com/dictionary/all.
ix. "Gonna." In *Merriam-Webster Dictionary*, n.d. https://www.merriam-webster.com/dictionary/gonna.
x. "Be." In *Merriam-Webster Dictionary*, July 25, 2025. https://www.merriam-webster.com/dictionary/be.
xi. "OK." In *Merriam-Webster Dictionary*, n.d. https://www.merriam-webster.com/dictionary/okay.

16. NOTES FROM YEAR 8

i. [1] Scripture promising we will be with Him forever and to the end of time.
ii. [2] Scripture for, I ask for eyes to see it, ears to hear it, and a heart to understand and receive the goodness, and love of God.
iii. 1 John 4:18 (*New King James Version*): "There is no fear in love; but perfect love casts out fear, because fear involves torment. But he who fears has not been made perfect in love."

Acknowledgments

Shari, thank you for believing in this book and in me, long before I had any clue of what it would require of each of us to complete it. Sister Annie, Shannon, Shiela, Carrie, and Barbara, your relentless love and support for the truth being told has bolstered my strength and willingness to just try. And then try again. My beautiful niece Kayleigh, thank you for thoughtfully, gently taking a million pics of me, knowing one of them would go on this cover. Thank you, mom and dad, for loving us and our babies so well, for holding on to us and to each other through the storms of life. Rich and Kathy, Mark and Gail, Colleen and Ryan, Jeanette and Kevin, thank you for loving us in the roughest of spots and for continuing to do so. Thank you, mommas and dadios, for wearing the same ugly shoes...thank you for your warmth, safety, and understanding all these years. Jeff, thank you. Thank you for encouraging me to stand. Thank you for loving me and our babies. Belle and Zo, thank you for sharing your incredible lives with me. I am so honored to be your mom, mama. Thank you, Gian, for living a beautiful life, for our budding friendship, for the gold you left for me to find. I love being your momma. Father God, thank You. Thank You for loving me in my heartsmash. Thank You for the beauty that is coming from it.

About the Author

Alanna King is a wife, mother of three grown children, and Nonni to three grands. She speaks in Arizona to high schoolers and court-ordered attendees on the power of our choices. Alanna is passionate and driven to find the gold in the hearts of those she encounters.

 facebook.com/alanna.king2

 instagram.com/heavenly_minded_momma

www.ingramcontent.com/pod-product-compliance
Lightning Source LLC
LaVergne TN
LVHW091043080826
845145LV00002B/609

* 9 7 8 1 7 3 3 5 3 5 8 4 7 *